I0829660

# Journal
# of
# The Hessian Jäger Corps
# 1777-1779

# Translated by
# W Steedman and Ian Saberton
# and
# Edited by Ian Saberton

Hessian foot jägers in action

# Journal
## of
## The Hessian Jäger Corps
## 1777-1779

Translated by
W Steedman and Ian Saberton
and
Edited by Ian Saberton

Grosvenor House
Publishing Limited

This book is published by
Grosvenor House Publishing Ltd
Link House
140 The Broadway, Tolworth, Surrey, KT6 7HT.
www.grosvenorhousepublishing.co.uk
info@grosvenorhousepublishing.co.uk



A CIP record for this book
is available from the British Library

ISBN 978-1-78623-336-3

# Acknowledgements

We are grateful to the staff of the Hessisches Staatsarchiv, Marburg, for courteously dealing with our various requests for assistance.

We are particularly indebted to Michelle Gantert and Stephen J. Dickens for meticulously checking the text and pertinently commenting on it.

Last but not least, our thanks go to Bruce Saberton for his technical advice.

# Introduction

This work contains the more significant part of a wider journal kept by the Hessian Jäger Corps during the American Revolutionary War — a corps forming part of the German mercenary troops employed by the British. It is particularly interesting for its first-hand account of the jägers' involvement in the Philadelphia campaign, the occupation of Philadelphia, and the subsequent withdrawal across New Jersey to New York. Besides an English translation, the German text is provided.

At the start of the Philadelphia campaign the Jäger Corps comprised four companies of foot jägers — three Hessian and one Anspach — and one mounted company, in all 600 men. As their name implies, most were huntsmen and all were crack shots, being armed with rifles, not muskets. While at Philadelphia the Corps was augmented by two newly arrived companies from Germany, increasing the total complement to 900, but it had suffered materially by attrition. For example, in the Battle of Brandywine two officers and six men were killed, whereas three sergeants and 35 privates were seriously wounded, the former of whom and many of the latter died. And so the losses continued during the numerous minor actions in which the Corps was engaged. The élite of the Hessian troops, the jägers were employed to great advantage in leading the van of a marching army or protecting its rear, covering a withdrawal, reconnoitring, and conducting partisan warfare, particularly ambuscades.

# Journal

## geführt

## Bey dem hochlöblich. Hessischen Feld-Jäger Corps

## während

## denen Campagnen der königl. Grossbrittanischen Armee in North America

## 1777-1779

# Journal

## kept by

## The Hessian Jäger Corps

## during

## The Campaigns of the Royal Army of Great Britain in North America

## 1777-1779

# ∞ 1777 ∞

*Juny 23*

Der Oberstlieutenant von Wurmb vom hochlöblichen LeibGarderegiment übernahm heute das Commando über das hochlöbliche Feld-Jäger Corps. Selbiges bestand nunmehro aus der Eskadron, so noch unberitten, und der Compagnie Major von Prueschenk, welche beyde soeben aus Europa angekommen waren, und denen Compagnien Ewald und von Wrede, welche die verwichene Campagne schon mitgemacht, nebst einer Compagnie Anspacher Jägers von 105 Mann unterm Capitaine von Crammond — das ganze im allem 600 Man ausmachend — wozu noch ein Detachment von 1 Offr. und 30 Mann hessischer Grenadiers kamen, welche die an das Corps attachierte zwey 3 pf. Canonen bedienten.

Die Armee war von Braunschweig zurückgekommen und stand ¾ Stunden von Amboy in Lager. Die feindliche stand bey Morris Town.

*Juny 24*

Alles ruhig. Nur einige feindliche Patrouillen liessen sich vor den Posten des Jäger Corps sehen.

*Juny 25*

Wir erhielten Ordre um 6 Uhr Abends die Zelte ab zubrechen und marschfähig zu seyn. Gegen 6 Uhr Abends wurde das Jäger Corps, so dazumal nur 400 Mann zum Dienst hatte, von 400 zu Fuss and 120 Mann zu Pferde auf seinem Posten attaquiert, schlug aber den Feind zurück

# ∞ 1777 ∞

*June 23*

Lt. Colonel von Wurmb of the Life Guards Regiment today assumed command of the Jäger Corps. It now consisted of the Squadron, as yet unmounted, and Major von Prueschenk's company, both of which had just arrived from Europe, and the companies of Ewald and von Wreden, which had already taken part in the previous campaign, together with a company of Anspach jägers, 105 strong, under Captain von Cramon — in all amounting to 600 men. In addition, there was a detachment of one officer and thirty Hessian grenadiers who attended the two 3-pounders attached to the Corps.

The army had returned from Brunswick and was encamped three quarters of an hour from Amboy. The enemy army was at Morristown.

*June 24*

Everything was halted. Only a few enemy patrols were spotted before the outposts of the Jäger Corps.

*June 25*

At six o'clock in the evening we received orders to strike the tents and to be ready to march. Towards six o'clock in the evening the Jäger Corps, which at the time had only 400 men for duty, was attacked at its post by 400 men on foot and 120 men on horseback, but we repulsed the enemy

ohne einen Verlust zu haben, ausser dass sich ein Mann selbst erschoss. Der Feind liess einige Todte zurück und wir machten verschiedene Gefangene.

*Juny 26*

Die feindliche Armee war bis Basketreach vorgerückt, um der unsrigen bey dem Übergang nach Staatenisland in die Arrière zu fallen. Die königliche Armee marschierte dahero mit Tages-Anbruch in zwey Colonnen, um den Feind zu attaquieren. Die Colonne rechts cammandiert von Lord Cornwallis und der Oberst Lt. von Wurmb mit der Compagnie von Prueschenk und v. Wrede machte dabey die Avantgarde, auf welche die light Infantry folgte. Bey der Colonne links war der General Howe, wo der Major von Prueschenk mit der Compagnie Ewald und denen Anspachern die Avantgarde machte. Verschiedene Scharmützel fielen bey der Colonne rechter Hand vor. Die Jägers und light Infanterie vertrieben den Feind von einigen Höhen ohne grossen Verlust, indem die light Infanterie nur einige Todte und blessierte hatte, u. die englische Garde und das Grenadier Bat. von Menigeroda attaquierten einen feindlichen Posten und erstere nahmen 1 and letztere 2 Canonen weg. Des Abends lagerte sich die Armee bey Westfield. General Howe recognoscierte das feindliche Lager zu Basketreach und fand es zu stark, weswegen er

*Juny 27*

mit der Armee bis Raway zurückmarschierte. Der Feind folgte nur in kleinen Partheyen nach, und da der Marsch sehr fatiguant und die Hizze ausserordentlich gross war, so verlohren wir verschiedene Menschen, die vor Hizze starben, besonders 4 Mann von der Eskadron, welche zu Fusse mit marschiert waren.

without loss except for one man who shot himself.  The enemy left a few dead and we took several prisoners.

*June 26*

The enemy army had advanced to Basketreach to fall on the rear of our own during the crossing to Staten Island. The royal army therefore marched at daybreak in two columns to attack the enemy.  The column on the right was commanded by Lord Cornwallis.  Lt. Colonel von Wurmb formed the van with von Prueschenk's company and von Wreden's and was followed by the light infantry.  General Howe was with the column on the left, where Major von Prueschenk formed the van with Ewald's company and the Anspachers.  The right-hand column was involved in various skirmishes.  The jägers and light infantry drove the enemy from a few heights without great loss — the light infantry having only a few dead and wounded — and the British Guards and the Grenadier Battalion von Minnigerode attacked an enemy post with the former capturing one, and the latter two, cannon.  In the evening the army camped at Westfield.  General Howe reconnoitred the enemy camp at Basketreach but found it too strong.  He therefore

*June 27*

marched back with the army to Rahway.  The enemy followed only in small parties, and as the march was very fatiguing and the heat extraordinarily great, we lost several men who died from the heat, in particular four men of the Squadron who had marched with us on foot.

*Juny 28*

Die Armee marschierte heute nach Amboy, und da der General beschlossen hatte diese ruinierte Provinz zu verlassen, so gingen schon diesen Nachmittag einige Trouppen nach Staatenisland über.

*Juny 29*

Die Armee beschäftigte sich heute mit dem Übergang nach Staatenisland. Der Feind war dabey ruhig.

*Juny 30*

Die Arrière Garde der Armee bestehend aus denen Grenadiers, light Infanterie und Jägers verliessen heute völlig die Provinz Jersey ohne beunruhigt zu werden und lagerte sich bey der Armee auf Staatenisland.

*July 1*

Die Armee rückte auf denen Höhen von Staatenisland ins Lager, ihr rechter Flügel gegen den Flaggstaff, und erhielt Ordre sich zu einer Seereise mit Provision zu versehen und zum Embarquement parat zu seyn.

*July 9*

Heute gingen die letzten Trouppen an board derer Transport Schiffe, wodurch sich das Embarquement endigte, dem ohngeachtet lag die Flotte mit denen Trouppen an board bis solche allererst

*July 20*

die Anker lichtete und nach Sandyhook segelte. Hier ankerte selbe wieder, damit alles was dazu gehöre zusammen kommen könne.

*June 28*

Today the army marched to Amboy and this afternoon some troops were already crossing to Staten Island, for the General had decided to leave this ruined province.

*June 29*

Today the army was occupied with crossing to Staten Island. The enemy meanwhile was quiet.

*June 30*

Today the rearguard of the army, consisting of the grenadiers, light infantry and jägers, left the Province of Jersey completely, without being molested, and encamped with the army on Staten Island.

*July 1*

The army moved into camp on the heights of Staten Island with its right wing against Fort Flagstaff[1] and received orders to lay in provisions for a voyage and to be ready for embarkation.

*July 9*

Today the last troops went on board the transport ships, thereby completing the embarkation.

*July 20*

The fleet nevertheless lay with the troops on board until 20 July, when it first weighed anchor and sailed to Sandy Hook. Here it anchored again to enable everything belonging to it to assemble.

*July 21 und 22*

War der wind contrair und konnten deswegen nicht auslaufen.

*July 23*

Wir liefen diesen Morgen mit einem günstigen Wind aus und nahmen unseren Cours nach dem Delaware, so wie man vermuthet. Wir hatten gutes Wetter aber nicht die besten Winde — erreichten auch die Mündung des Delaware

*July 30*

und glaubten gewiss, dass wir zu Newcastle landen würden, allein wir kamen nicht weiter als Cap Henlopen, wo wir den *Roebuck* von 40 Canonen (Sir Snape Hammond) auf seiner dasigen Station antraffen.

*July 31*

Verliess die Flotte zu unserer aller Verwunderung die Bay des Delaware and ging in See. Sir Snape Hammond soll dieses verursacht haben, indem er behauptet, dass die Gegend von New Castle zu gefährlich läge und dass daselbst die Flotte zu sehr denen vielen feindlichen Feuerschiffen ausgesetzt sey. Die Flotte nahm ihren Cours gegen die Chesapeak Bay, welches gewöhnlich eine zwey tätige Reise ist. Die widrigen Winde aber hielten uns auf bis

*August 15*

wo die Flotte zu Cape Henry vor Anker kam.

*July 21 and 22*

The wind was contrary and so we could not sail.

*July 23*

This morning we put to sea with a favourable wind and set course, so we assume, for the Delaware. We had good weather but not the best of winds. We did reach the mouth of the Delaware

*July 30*

and were convinced we would land at New Castle, but we got no farther than Cape Henlopen, where we fell in with the *Roebuck* of 40 guns (Sir Andrew Snape Hamond[2]) at her station there.

*July 31*

To the surprise of us all, the fleet left Delaware Bay and steered out to sea. Sir Andrew Snape Hamond is said to have been the cause of this, for he claimed that the New Castle area was too dangerous and that the fleet would be too exposed there to the many enemy fire-ships. The fleet set course for Chesapeake Bay, which is usually a two-day voyage, but the contrary winds delayed us until

*August 15*

when the fleet anchored off Cape Henry.

*August 16*

Ankerten wir vor Milford.

*August 17*

Bey Queen's Island.

*August 18*

Ohnweit von Smiths Point.

*August 19*

Bey Cedar Point.

*August 20*

Zwischen Wards und Sharps Island.

*August 21*

Bey Bodkins Point.

*August 22*

Ohnweit Turkey Point, George Town gegenüber, und zwar so nahe am Lande der Chester-County, dass die Flotte sehr leicht hätte können beschossen werden.

*August 23 und 24*

Wurden die nöthigen Vorkehrungen zum Debarquement getroffen.

*August 16*

We anchored off Milford.[3]

*August 17*

Off Gwynn's Island.[4]

*August 18*

Near Smith's Point.[5]

*August 19*

Off Cedar Point.[6]

*August 20*

Between Ward's and Sharp's Islands.[7]

*August 21*

Off Bodkin's Point.[8]

*August 22*

Near Turkey Point, opposite George Town, and so near to land in Chester County that the fleet could very easily have been fired upon.

*August 23 and 24*

The necessary preparations were made for disembarkation.

*August 25*

Heute früh 3 Uhr fing sich das Debarquement in folgender Ordnung an:

|  |  |
|---|---|
|  | Das Jäger Corps *à la tête* |
| 1stes Debarquement | 1stes und 2tes Bat. light Infantry |
|  | 1stes und 2tes Bat englischer Grenadiers |
| 2te Debarquation | Hessische Grenadiers, Queens Rangers, englische Garde, 4tes und 23tes Regiment |
| 3te Debarquation | 28, 49, 5, 10, 27, 40, 55, 15, 42tes Regmt |
| 4te Debarquation | 44, 17, 33, 37, 46, 64 und 71tes Rgmt. |
| 5te Debarquation | Leib Regmt, v. Donop, Mirbach, combiniert Bataillon, Artillerie und Cavallerie der Armee. |

Die Landung geschah an und vor sich in der besten Ordnung auf Elk Ferry auf Turkey Point (ist eine Erdzunge, so einen einzigen schmalen Ausgang nach Elktown, einem kleinen Städtgen von ohngefähr 40 Häusern an dem Flusse dieses Namens, hat). Sobald die erste Division an Land tratt, und da man keine feindliche Nachricht hatte, formierten sich die Leute gleich Compagnieweise, ohne Rücksicht auf Enciennité, um sich dem sich allenfalls nähernden Feinde zu widersezzen und die Landung der ganzen Armee zu decken. So liess sich aber nichts vom Feinde sehen.

*August 26 und 27*

Blieb die Armee stehen, um ihre nötige Baggage an Land zu bringen und alles zum Marsch fertig zu machen.

*August 25*

Early today, at three o'clock in the morning,[9] disembarkation began in the following order:

|  |  |
|---|---|
|  | The Jäger Corps *à la tête* |
| 1st disembarkation | 1st and 2nd battalions light infantry |
|  | 1st and 2nd battalions British Grenadiers |
| 2nd disembarkation | Hessian Grenadiers, Queen's Rangers, British Guards, 4th and 23rd Regiments |
| 3rd disembarkation | 28th, 49th, 5th, 10th, 27th, 40th, 55th, 15th, and 42nd Regiments |
| 4th disembarkation | 44th, 17th, 33rd, 37th, 46th, 64th and 71st Regiments |
| 5th disembarkation | Leib Regiment, von Donop, Mirbach, combined battalion, artillery and cavalry of the army. |

The landing as such went off in excellent order at Elk Ferry on Turkey Point (a spit of land with only one narrow exit to Elk Town, a small town of some 40 houses on the river of the same name). As soon as the first division set foot on land, there being no news of the enemy, the men immediately formed into companies, regardless of seniority, in order to oppose the enemy if they should approach and to cover the landing of the whole army. However, nothing was seen of the enemy.

*August 26 and 27*

The army was halted so as to disembark such baggage as was needed and to get everything ready for marching.

Die Armee brach von Turkey Point auf und marschierte nach Elktown, welcher Ort von allen Einwohnern verlassen war. Vom Feinde hatten wir keine Nachricht und keine Karte vom Innern des Landes und in der Armee war niemand der diese Gegend kannte. Nachdem wir also die Stadt passiert, wusste nun niemand weiter einen Weg. Es wurde dahero aller Orten herumgeschickt bis sich endlich ein Negroe fandt, nach dessen gegebener Beschreibung die Armee marschieren musste. Dieser Negroe wusste zwar nichts von der fiendl. Armee selbst, sagte aber, dass ein Corps derselben in der Nähe sey, von welchem sich auch Observations Partheyen von dem Jäger Corps, das die Avantgarde machte, sehen liessen. Die Armee bezog ein Lager in denen Wäldern. Das Jäger Corps für den linken Flügel derselben an dem Fuss eines Berges, die leichte Infanterie war auf dem selbigen postiert. Hier blieben wir bis zum 3ten September liegen und machten inzwischen einige Gefangene von der sich öfter zeigenden Observations Parthey, welche uns benachrichtigten, dass die feindl. Armee nicht in der Nähe sey (wie wir selbst vermutheten), wohl aber dass ein Corps von 1,200 auserlesener Mannschaft zu Ironhill stehe (dieses ist der höchste Berg von der Chesapeake Bay bis Philadelphia).

*September 3*

General Major Grand blieb mit 6 Bat. zu Elk, um die Communication mit denen Schiffen zu erhalten. Lord Cornwallis Colonne brach mit Tages Anbruch auf und marschierte nach Cecil Court House, wo sich der Gen. Lt. v. Knyphausen mit ihr vereinigte. Die Jägers (bestehend aus der Comp. Prueschenk, v. Wrede, Ewald und Anspach, in allem etwas über 400 Mann) machten die Avantgarde und fanden

*August 28*

The army set off from Turkey Point and marched to Elk Town, which had been deserted by all its inhabitants. We had no news of the enemy, no map of the interior of the country, and there was no one in the army who knew this area. So, after we had passed the town, no one knew a way forward. Therefore men were sent all around till at length a black man was found, and the army had to march from the description that he gave. This black man knew nothing of the enemy army itself but said that there was a corps belonging to it in the vicinity. Observation parties from this corps were also spotted by the Jäger Corps, which was forming the van. The army camped in the woods. The Jäger Corps was on the left wing of the army at the foot of a hill while the light infantry was posted on the hill itself. We remained here till 3 September and meanwhile we captured a few of the observation party, which was frequently showing itself. They informed us that the enemy army was not in the vicinity (as we ourselves surmised) but that there was possibly a corps of 1,200 picked men at Iron Hill (the highest mountain between Chesapeake Bay and Philadelphia).

*September 3*

Maj. Gen. Grant[10] remained at Elk with six battalions to maintain the communication with the ships. Lord Cornwallis's column set off at daybreak and marched to Cecil Court House, where Lt. Gen. von Knyphausen joined them. The jägers (consisting of von Prueschenk's, von Wreden's, Ewald's and the Anspach companies — in all, something over 400 men) formed the van and discovered during the march that the enemy pickets had been there before us and that, according to their tracks, the enemy had marched to the left. Colonel von Wurmb reported this and sought

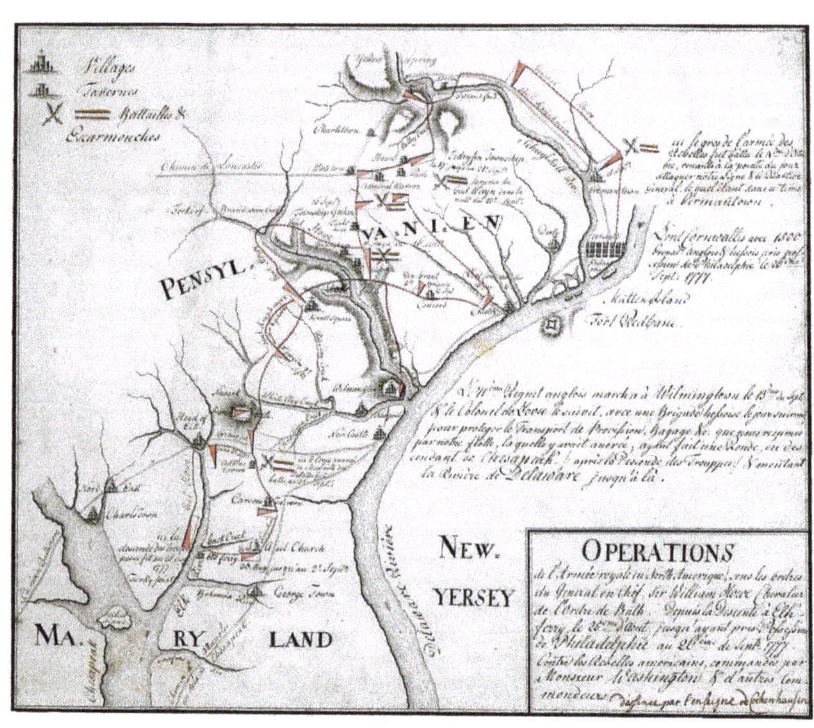

Hessian map of the Philadelphia campaign

**Present-day map of the Philadelphia campaign**

während des Marsches, dass die feindl. Picquets da gewesen und dass, der Spur nach, der Feind links marschiert sey. Der Oberst von Wurmb liess dieses melden und bat um Befehl welchen Weg er marschieren soll. Sir Wm Howe kam selbst und befahl der feindl. Spur zu folgen. Nach ½ Stundt sahen unsere Blänkers die feindl. Arrière. Die berittenen Jägers attaquierten solche folglich und der Capt. Ewald, der die Avantgarde des Corps machte, kam gleichwohl bald ins Feuer. Wir sahen darauf den Feind, in ohngefähr 1,000 Mann bestehend, in einem lichten Walde aufmarschiert. Das Jäger Corps deployierte aus der Mitte rechts und links und formierte sich so, dass die Anspacher die Mitte hatten, in welcher Stellung der Feind sogleich attaquierte und mit vieler Mühe in einen anderen Wald zurückgeschlagen wurde. Hier vertheitigte er sich hartnäckig, weswegen dann auch unser rechter Flügel unter Capt. Wrede mit den Hirschfängern attaquierte. Wir vertrieben ihn auch aus dieser Stellung und er nahm eine dritte hinter der Catcher's Brücke, dies aber bloss um seine Retraite besser zu decken, in dem er sich in einen dichten Wald retirierte, ohne weiteren Stand zu halten. Hier und nachdem der Feind schon würklich retiriert war, kam erst ein Bat. leichte Infanterie zu uns, das der General Howe rechts detachiert hatte um uns zu unterstützen, wegen einem Morast aber nicht hatte durchkommen können, und das 2te Bat., welches links detachiert gewesen, konnte wegen einem grossen Sumpf gar nicht zu uns kommen — so dass also das Jäger Corps dieses feindliche *Corps de tête* ganz alleine schlugen, weshalb auch der commandierende General dem Oberst Lt. von Wurmb and dem ganzen Corps bey der Parole seinen besten Dank abstattete. Wir begruben zwischen 30 und 40 Todte vom Fiende, ohne was in den Büschen versteckt blieb. Unsere Verluste waren 1 Todt und 15 blessierte Hessen u. 4 blessierte Anspacher. Die Armee ging darauf ins Lager. Die Jägers hatten ihren Posten für den linken Flügel in einem sehr angenehmen aber exponierten Wald.

orders as to which way he should march. Sir William Howe came in person and ordered the enemy's tracks to be followed. After half an hour our skirmishers[11] spotted the enemy's rear. The mounted jägers therefore attacked it, and Captain Ewald, who formed the van of the Corps, soon came under fire. We then saw the enemy, consisting of some 1,000 men, drawn up in an open wood. The Jäger Corps deployed from the centre to the right and left and formed so that the Anspachers held the centre, in which position the enemy attacked at once and were driven back into another wood with much difficulty. Here they defended stubbornly, so our right wing under Captain von Wreden attacked with the hunting knives. We did drive them from this position and they took up a third behind Cooch's Bridge, but only so as to cover their retreat better, retiring, as they did, into a dense wood without making a further stand. Here, and only after the enemy had actually retired, were we first joined by a battalion of light infantry which General Howe had detached on the right to support us but which had been unable to get through because of a morass, whilst the 2nd battalion, which had been detached on the left, was unable to get to us at all owing to a large swamp. Thus the Jäger Corps defeated this enemy *corps de tête* all on its own, for which the GOC conveyed in General Orders[12] his profound thanks to Lt. Colonel von Wurmb and the entire Corps. We buried between thirty and forty enemy dead without counting what remained hidden in the bushes. Our losses were one dead and fifteen Hessians wounded and four Anspachers wounded. The army then encamped. The jägers had their post on the left wing in a very pleasant but exposed wood.

Ein Capitain und womöglich 2 Subalterns mit 70 auch manigmal 100 und mehrere Männer hatten jezzo (und während denen ganzen Campagnen) die verschiedenen Picquets des Corps und diese machten bey vorkommenden Märschen jedes mal die Avant- oder Arrière Garde und wurden alle 24 Stunden abgelöst. Das Corps selbst wurde öfters des Nachts durch falsche oder reale Lärmen alarmiert und musste öfters unters Gewehr tretten, weswegen auch ein jeder Jäger, so er im Gliede standt, mit seiner Büchse sich niederlegen musste, um jedes malen mit dem geringsten Lärm folglich parat zu stehen, welches denn auch nachher, bey aller und jeder Gelegenheit, niemalen fahlschlug. Die Cavallerie campierte jedesmal in einer gewissen Distance hinter der Infanterie und war gesattelt und grossenteils aufgestangt.

Die Zelter und schwere Bagage der Armee wurden von hier aus an die Schiffe gebracht.

*September 6*

General Major Grand mit denen 6 Bataillons vereinigte sich mit der Armee. Die königl. Flotte hatte den Elk Fluss verlassen und die jenigen feindl. Fahrzeuge daselbst verbrannt, welche nicht weg gebracht werden konnten.

*September 8*

Die fiendl. Armee war bis Newarck vorgerückt und zwar solcher gestalt gelagert, dass deren rechter Flügel an den Christian Creek und der linke an Red Clay Creek stosse und vielmehr davon gedeckt wurde. Die Armee marschierte dahero heute in folgender Ordnung:

> 1ste Division, Lord Cornwallis: Jägers, 1stes u. 2tes Bat. light Infantry, englische Grenadiers, hessische Grenadiers, Garde

A captain, and if possible two subalterns, with seventy or sometimes a hundred or more men, formed now (and during all the campaigns) the various pickets of the Corps, and on marches they always formed the van or the rearguard, being relieved every twenty-four hours.  At night the Corps itself was often turned out on real or false alarms and had frequently to be under arms, so that each jäger forming in the ranks had to lie down with his rifle and be ever ready on the slightest alarm — which never failed, now or later, on any occasion.  The cavalry always camped a certain distance behind the infantry and were always saddled and to a large extent bitted.[13]

The tents and heavy baggage of the army were taken from here to the ships.

*September 6*

Maj. Gen. Grant with the six battalions joined up with the army.  The royal fleet had left Elk River and had burnt those enemy vessels there that could not be removed.

*September 8*

The enemy army had advanced to Newark and had camped with its right wing on Christina Creek, and the left on Red Clay Creek, and was covered by them.  The army therefore marched today in the following order:

> 1st Division, Lord Cornwallis: Jägers, 1st and 2nd battalions light infantry, British Grenadiers, Hessian Grenadiers, Guards

2te Division, General Major Grand: 2 Escadrons 16 Dragoner, erste Brigade Artillerie, 1ste u. 2te Brigade englishche Infanterie, 3e Brigade Artillerie, 3te u. 4te Brigade engl. Infanterie, hierauf der Trein der Armee

3e Division, Gen. Lt. v. Knyphausen: Die unberittenen Jägers der Escadron, 2e Brigade Artillerie, General Sterns Brigade, 1 Escadron 16 Dragoner, 40 Rgmt., 2 3 lb, 71 Rgmt., die Queens Rangers und engl. Jägers.

Das 3e Bat. des 71 Rgmts stellte die rechte Flanque der Bagage. Am Abend lagerte sich die Armee auf der Strasse nach Newarck ohnferne Hockensen, folglich in einer Entfernung von 4 Meilen vom Feind.

*September 9*

Der Feind hatte gestern und verwichene Nacht eine Bewegung auf der Strasse nach Wilmington gemacht, war über den Brandewine Creek bis Chadsfurth gegangen, und hatte sich auf dessen Höhen postiert, auch angefangen Redutten aufzuwerfen. Diese Bewegung mochte die der königlichen Armee nach sich ziehen, in dem der General Lieutenant von Knyphausen nach Newgarden und Kennetsquare und Lord Cornwallis nach Hockensen Meetinghouse marschierten und beyde vereinigten sich

*September 10*

des nächsten Morgens bey Kennetsquare.

*September 11*

Bey Tages Anbruch marschierte die Armee in 2 Colonnen. Die rechte unterm General Lieutenant v. Knyphausen, mit Imbegriff der Division des General Major Grand, nahm die

2nd Division, Major Gen. Grant: 2 Squadrons 16th Dragoons, 1st Artillery Brigade, 1st and 2nd Brigades British infantry, 3rd Artillery Brigade, 3rd and 4th Brigades British infantry, then the army's train

3rd Division, Lt. Gen. von Knyphausen: The unmounted jägers of the Squadron, 2nd Artillery Brigade, General Stirn's Brigade, 1 Squadron 16th Dragoons, 40th Regiment, two 3-pounders, 71st Regiment, the Queen's Rangers, and British chasseurs.[14]

The 3rd Battalion of the 71st Regiment covered the right flank of the baggage. In the evening the army camped on the road to Newark, not far from Hockessin and at a distance of four miles from the enemy.

### September 9

Yesterday and last night the enemy had been in motion on the road to Wilmington, had gone across Brandywine Creek to Chadd's Ford, taken post on the heights there, and had started to throw up redoubts. This movement may have drawn the royal army's after it, for Lt. Gen. von Knyphausen marched to New Garden and Kennett Square, Lord Cornwallis to Hockessin Meetinghouse, and both joined up

### September 10

next morning at Kennett Square.

### September 11

At daybreak the army marched in two columns. The right under Lt. Gen. von Knyphausen, which included Maj. Gen. Grant's division, took the road to Chadd's Ford, seven miles

Strasse nach Chadsfurth 7 Meilen von Kennetsquare und kam um 10 Uhr vor der feindlichen Front daselbst an. Die Avantgarde dieser Colonne bestehend in denen Queens Rangers harangierte mit denen feindlichen Vorposten während des Anmarsches, und da der General v. Knyphausen nicht eher attaquieren wollte bis ihn die linke Colonne unter Sir Wm Howe und Lord Cornwallis auf dessen rechten Flügel angreifen würde, so amusierte er den Feind nur mit Artilleriefeuer, also ob er die Furth zu forcieren willens sey. Sir Wm Howe marschierte inzwischen bis nach dem ersten Arm des Brandewine Creek (eine Distance von 12 Meilen), Das Jäger Corps machte die Avantgarde dieser Colonne und wurde durch das 1ste u. 2te Bat. leichte Infanterie (Oberst Lt. Abercrombie) unterstützt, auf welche die Grenadiers folgten. Der Capt. Ewald mit 50 Jägers (unterstützt von Capt. Scott mit seiner Comp. light Infanterie) hatte den äussersten Posten vor dem Jäger Corps. Ohngefähr 2 Meilen diesseits des Brandewine hielten wir eine feindliche Patrouille von 100 Mann an, welche sich mit Zurücklassung einiger Gefangener in Wald retirierte, und diese war es, so den General Washington von unserem Anmarsch auf diesem Wege informierte und ihn bewog, seine bisherige Meynung, dass die Armee bey Chatsfurth würklich übergehen wolle, zu ändern, und mit dem grössten Theil seiner Armee engegen zu detachieren. Wir gingen unterdessen über den ersten Arm des Brandewine Creek durch Finckloss's Furth und über den zweyten bey Jeffery's Furth. Hier war ein höher Berg, dass 500 Mann mit 2 Canonen den Übergang darüber hatten, wo nicht unmöglich doch wenigstens äusserst schwer, machen können, und da dieser nicht besetzt war, so bestärkte sich der commandierende General in seiner Meynung, dass Washington sich retirieren und keine Bataille liefern würde, und dass es nicht an dem sey, dass er von Congress positive Ordre sich zu schlagen habe. Es war äusserst mühsam die Artillerie über diesen Berg zu bringen,

from Kennet Square, and at ten o'clock came before the enemy's front there. The van of this column, consisting of the Queen's Rangers, skirmished with the enemy's advanced posts during the advance, and as General von Knypausen was not about to attack until the left-hand column under Sir William Howe and Lord Cornwallis attacked the right wing of the enemy, he merely amused the enemy with artillery fire as if he was minded to force the ford. Meanwhile Sir William Howe marched to the first arm of Brandywine Creek (a distance of 12 miles). The Jäger Corps formed the van of this column and was supported by the 1st and 2nd battalions light infantry (Lt. Colonel Abercromby), followed by the Grenadiers. Captain Ewald with fifty jägers (supported by Captain Scott[15] and his company of light infantry) had the outermost position ahead of the Jäger Corps. About two miles from the Brandywine we intercepted an enemy patrol of one hundred men, who retired into the woods, leaving behind some prisoners. It was they who informed General Washington of our advance along this route, and who induced him not only to change his former opinion that the army really intended to cross at Chadd's Ford but also to detach the greater part of his army against us. Meanwhile we crossed the first arm of Brandywine Creek through Finglas's Ford and crossed the second at Jeffrey's Ford. Here was a hill so high that, though it was not impossible to do so, 500 men with two cannon were able to cross it only with extreme difficulty. As it was not occupied, it confirmed the GOC in his opinion that Washington would retire and not give battle and that it was not true he had been given a positive order by Congress to fight. Getting the artillery over this hill was extremely laborious, so the column halted on the other side of it until two o'clock. After the artillery had been brought over and we had set off marching in column through a landscape which was rather open for this part of the country, Captain Ewald reported

weshalb auch die Colonne jenseits desselben bis 2 Uhr halt machte. Nachdem nun die Artillerie herüber gebracht und wir uns in einer, dem hiesigen Lande nach, ziemlich offenen Gegend *en Colonne* in Marsch setzten, liess der Capt. Ewald gegen 3 Uhr melden, dass die fiendl. Armee gegen uns in Anmarsch sey. Hierauf erhielten wir dann Ordre die Linie zu formieren u. die Avantgarde deployierte aus der Mitte rechts und links. Das Jäger Corps hatte die Ehre den äussersten linken Flügel zu erhalten und bestand nach Abzug des Detachments unter Capt. Ewald und der Cavallerie, so wegen dem difficilen Terrain nicht folgen konnte, in etwas über 300 Mann mit 2 englischen 3 lb, die der Lieut. Merz mit 30 Grenadiers zwar deckte, im avancieren aber mit denen Grenadiers zurücklassen musste. Rechts dem Jäger Corps waren 2 Bat. leichten Infanterie, das Centrum hatten die Infanterie Regimenter, und den rechten Flügel die Garde und Grenadiers. Die hessischen Grenadiers unterstützten den rechten Flügel u. die 3e Brigade Engländer sollte ebenwohl die Jägers und leichte Infanterie im 2ten Treffen soutenieren, solche blieb aber wegen dem zu sehr coupierten Terrain und dem links ziehen der Colonne zurück und wir sahen nichts von ihr während der Bataille. Gegen halb 4 Uhr fand sich das Jäger Corps nahe an einem feindlichen avancierten Posten mit 2 6 lb und 600 Mann, welche auf einer Anhöhe standen u. einen Wald vor sich hatten. Unsere 2 3 lb eröffneten das erste Feuer. Die Jägers attaquierten diesen Feind, trieben ihn in einen Werck, und delogierten ihn zu 3 verschiedenenmalen, ehe er sich auf das HauptCorps der Armee zurückzog. Diese war auf einer recht steilen Anhöhe vor einem Walde sehr vortheilhaft postiert und ihr rechter Flügel an einem steil und tiefen Ravin appuyiert. Die Jägers standen diesem Flügel gerade gegen über und zwar in demjenigen Werck, wo sie das avanciert gewesene feindlich. Corps zuletzt herausgetrieben hatten und waren dem feindlichen

towards three o'clock that the enemy army was advancing against us. We then received orders to form the line and the van deployed from the centre to the right and left. The Jäger Corps had the honour of receiving the extreme left wing, and after the detachment under Captain Ewald had been withdrawn, together with the cavalry, which could not follow due to the difficult terrain, it consisted of something over 300 men with two British 3-pounders. Lieutenant Mertz covered the cannon with thirty grenadiers, but on the advance he had to leave the cannon and grenadiers behind. On the right of the Jäger Corps were the two battalions of light infantry, the centre was formed by the infantry regiments, and the right wing by the Guards and Grenadiers. The Hessian Grenadiers supported the right wing. The 3rd British Brigade were to support both the jägers and light infantry as the second line,[16] but owing to the terrain, which was intersected too much, and to the marching of the column to the left, they remained behind and we saw nothing of them during the battle. Towards half past three the Jäger Corps found themselves near an enemy advanced post of two 6-pounders and 600 men who stood on rising ground with a wood in front of them. Our two 3-pounders opened fire first. The jägers attacked the enemy, drove them into a patch of woodland, and dislodged them on three separate occasions before they withdrew to the main corps of the army. This was posted very advantageously on a rather steep rise in front of a wood with its right wing resting on a steep and deep ravine. The jägers were directly opposite this wing, in the very woodland from which we had finally driven the advanced corps of the enemy, and together with the one battalion of light infantry we were exposed for more than half an hour to the enemy's grapeshot and small-arms fire. We were unable to observe the second battalion of light infantry owing to the terrain, for, as we

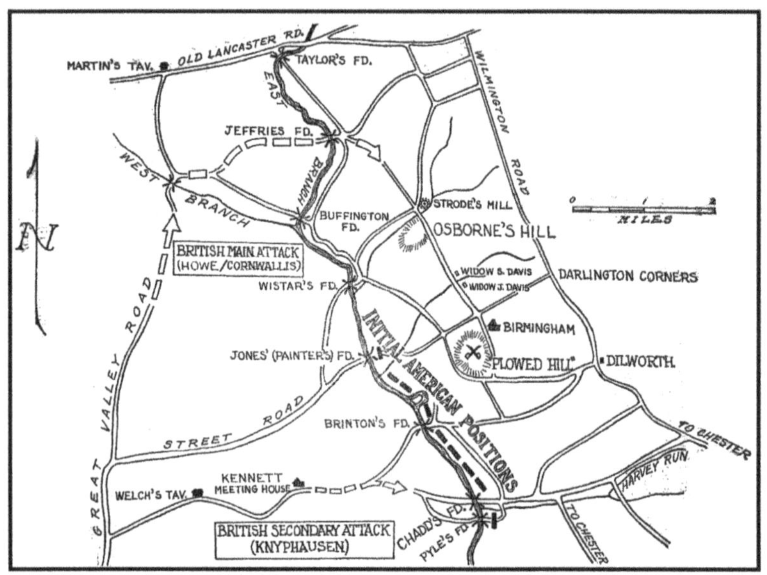


## The Battle of Brandywine
## 11 September 1777

Cartätschen und klein. Gewehrfeuer mit dem einen Bat. liechter Infanterie über ½ Stunde ausgesetzt. Das 2e Bat. leichte Infanterie konnten wir wegen dem Terrain nicht observieren, denn, da wir wenig ordres erhielten, so agierte ein jeder Commandeur nach gut dünken. Inzwischen wurde das Feuer algemein and heftiger und da der Oberstlt. von Wurmb hörte, dass es auf dem rechten Flügel avancierte, so liess er den Halbenmond zur Attaque blasen und die Jägers mit dem Bat. leichte Infanterie stürmten den Berg hinauf, worauf sich der Feind in Confusion in den Wald retirierte und uns 2 Canonen und ein Ammunitions Lager zurückliess, welche die leichte Infanterie, da sie an der weniger steilen Seite des Berges attaquiert hatte, in Besitz nahm.

Wir hatten keine Cavallerie, unsere Leute waren zu sehr fatiguiert, und der Feind in einem Augenblick aus unserem Gesicht, machten dahero auch keine Gefangene. Die Jägers hatten den Lieutenant von Forster von Anspach und 6 Man Todte nebst dem Capt. Trautwetter, 3 Sgt und 35 Gemeine schwer blessiert, wovon erstere nebst vielen der letzteren starben. Der Verlust des Bat. leichte Infanterie war nicht so stark und vom Feinde sahen wir viele Todte und blessierte. Dadurch dass das 2te Bat. leichte Infanterie zu weit rechts attaquiert hatte, waren wir ganz von der Armee abgesondert und stiessen erste gegen 7 Uhr Abends auf erhaltener Ordre zu selbiger zu Dalworth, wo sie auf dem *Champs de Bataille* gelagert war, ohne den Feind in seiner Retraite zu verfolgen.

General Lieutenant v. Knyphausen war, verabredeten Plan gemäss, sobald er das Feuer von uns gehört, durch Chadsfurth gegangen, hatte 3 Canonen und 1 Haubize von einer kleinen Redoutte erobert und den Feind gleichwohl in die Flucht geschlagen. Der Verlust der ganzen königl.

received few orders, every commander acted as he thought best. Meanwhile the fire became general and more intensive, and as Lt. Colonel von Wurmb heard that the right wing was advancing, he had the bugle-horn[17] sound the attack. The jägers and the battalion of light infantry stormed up the hill, whereupon the enemy retired into the wood in confusion, leaving behind for us two cannon and an ammunition store, which the light infantry took into their possession, for they had attacked on the side of the hill which was less steep.

We had no cavalry, our men were too fatigued, and the enemy were out of sight in the twinkling of an eye. We therefore took no prisoners. The jägers had Lieutenant von Forster from Anspach and six men killed, together with Captain Trautwetter. Three sergeants and thirty-five privates were seriously wounded, and the former and many of the latter died. The losses of the battalion of light infantry were not so severe and we saw many of the enemy's dead and wounded. As the 2nd battalion of light infantry had attacked too far to the right, we were completely separated from the army, and on receiving orders we rejoined them only towards seven o'clock in the evening at Dilworth, where they had encamped on the battlefield without pursuing the enemy on his retreat.

As soon as he heard our fire, Lt. Gen. von Knyphausen had crossed Chadd's Ford in accordance with the agreed plan, capturing three cannon and one howitzer from a small redoubt, and had forced the enemy to flee. The losses of the entire royal army are roughly 400 dead and wounded, whilst the enemy's are estimated to be 300 dead, 600 wounded, and 400 prisoners.

Armee ist zwishen 400 Todte und blessierte, der feindl.
hingegen rechnet man auf 300 Todte, 600 blessierte, und
400 Gefangene.

*September 12*

Gen. Howe stattete der Armee seine Danksagung über die
gestrige Bataille bey der Parole ab und erwähnte besonders
denen Trouppen, so die Avantgarde gehabt und den ersten
Angriff gethan hatte. Die Armee blieb zu unser aller
Verwunderung ruhig liegen, nur dass der General Major
Grand mit der 1sten and 2ten Brigade nach Concorde rückte.

*September 13*

Die Jägers mussten auf der linken Flanque der Armee
marschieren. Lord Cornwallis mit der leichten Infanterie
und denen Grenadiers vereinigte sich mit Gen. Maj. Grand
und rückte bis 5 Meilen von Chester vor, wo sich ein Theil
des Feindes retranchiert haben sollten. Das 71ste Regmt
wurde deswegen dahin detachiert, um solchen zu delogieren
und Posto au fassen, bey dessen Ankunft aber fand man den
Ort schon verlassen.

*September 14*

Die blessierten und Kranken der Armee gingen heute nach
Wilmington, wohin sie der Oberst von Loos mit dem
kombinierten Bataillon escortierte. Die Jägers machten
eine Patrouille nach Renny, machten daselbst einige
Gefangene, und ruinierten ein kleines Magazin.

*September 15*

Alles ruhig. Ordre am Morgen zu marschieren.

*September 12*

General Howe conveyed in General Orders his thanks to the army for their part in yesterday's battle and especially mentioned the troops who had formed the van and made the first attack. To the surprise of us all, the army remained motionless apart from Maj. Gen. Grant, who marched towards Concord with the 1st and 2nd Brigades.

*September 13*

The jägers had to march on the left flank of the army. Lord Cornwallis with the light infantry and the Grenadiers joined up with Maj. Gen. Grant and advanced until five miles from Chester, where part of the enemy were said to be entrenched. The 71st Regiment were accordingly detached there to dislodge them and to take post, but on their arrival the place was found to be already abandoned.

*September 14*

The army's wounded and sick went to Wilmington today and were escorted by Colonel von Loos and the combined battalion. The jägers made a patrol to The Warren Tavern, took a few prisoners there, and destroyed a small magazine.

*September 15*

Everything was halted. Orders to march tomorrow.

*September 16*

The Regiment von Mirbach marched to Wilmington to cover the hospital established there.

*September 16*

Das Rgmt. von Mirbach marschierte nach Wilmington, um das daselbst etablierte Hospital zu decken.

Die Armee marschierte links, um den General Washington, der denen erhaltenen Nachrichten zufolge auf der Strasse nach Lancaster marschierte, an zugreifen. Die Jägers und leichte Infanterie fielen auch würklich mit selbigen ein und hatten heftige Scharmützel. Vom Feinde wurden 1 Capitain, 1 Officier und 20 Mann gefangen und viele blieben auf dem Platze. Von unserer Seite blieb 1 Man Todt und einige wurden blessiert. Wegen dem ausser ordentlichen Regen-Wetter aber wurde der Marsch nicht fortgesetzt, sondern das Lager bey Butte aufgeschlagen, und der Feind, gleichwohl des Regens halber, hatte sich bey Black Horse gelagert und den Marsch aufgeschoben.

*September 17*

Die Colonne des General Howe blieb in Lager, Lord Cornwallis aber avancierte auf der Lancaster Strasse und fasste in der Entfernung von 2 Meilen von Gen. Lt. v. Knyphausen Posto.

*September 18*

Die Armee vereinigte sich heute auf der Lancaster Strasse beim Weissen Ross. Wir erfuhren, dass der Feind über den Skuyllkill gegangen und an diesem Fluss zu beyden Seiten des Peckgomy Bachs campierte.

*September 19*

Alles ruhig. Ordre morgen zu marschieren

The army marched to the left to attack General Washington, who, according to information received, was marching along the road to Lancaster. The jägers and light infantry did indeed fall in with them and had some savage skirmishes. Of the enemy one captain, one officer and twenty men were captured and many left for dead on the spot. For our part we had one man killed and several wounded. However, due to the extraordinarily rainy weather the march was not continued and camp was pitched at The Boot Tavern. The enemy had encamped at The Black Horse, postponing their march, also due to the rain.

*September 17*

General Howe's column remained in camp, but Lord Cornwallis advanced on the Lancaster road, taking post two miles distant from Lt. Gen. von Knyphausen.

*September 18*

Today the army joined up at The White Horse on the Lancaster road. We learned that the enemy had crossed the Schuylkill and encamped against this river on both sides of Perkiomen Creek.

*September 19*

Everything was halted. Orders to march tomorrow.

*September 20*

The army marched in the following order: jägers *à la tête*, light infantry, 1st, 2nd, 3rd and 4th British Brigades, Stirn's Hessian Brigade, Hessian Grenadiers and the Dragoons,

*September 20*

Die Armee marschierte in folgender Ordnung: jägers *à la tête*, leichte Infanterie, 1ste, 2te, 3te und 4te Brigade Engländer, hessische Brigade Stern, hessische Grenadiers und die Dragoner, welche so wie die Artillerie in Detachments *à la tête* derer Brigaden vertheilt wurden. Die Queens Rangers u. 2 Bat. Engländer deckten die Flanque. Das Jäger Corps scharmützelte ständig während des Marsches und das Lager wurde zu Valley Forge aufgeschlagen, wo verschiedene Magazine, eine Stück-Giesserei und eine Gewehr Fabrique ruiniert wurden.

*September 21*

Verwichene Nacht wurde General Major Gray mit der leichten Infanterie, 42 u. 44tes Rgmt. detachiert, um ein feindl. Corps unterm General Wayne zu überrumpeln, das in denen Waldungen ganz allein stehe und 1,500 Mann stark seye. Er erreichte den Feind um 1 Uhr des Nachts, brach in seine linke Flanque mit ungeladenen Gewehrs, tödtete und verwundete 300, machte 80 Gefangene und nahm den grössten Theil der Bagage weg, nebst vielen Gewehrs. Die Canonen aber hatte der Feind davon gebracht. Der engl. Verlust war 1 Capt., 3 Mann todt and 4 verwundet.

Die Armee brach sehr früh auf und marschierte in der folgenden Ordnung: jägers, leichte Infanterie, hessische Grenadiers, 3 Brigaden Artillerie, Bagage und Trein der Armee, die 4te, 2te, 1ste Brigade Engländer. Die 3e Brigade deckte die Flanque und die hessische Brigade machte die Arrière.

Der Marsch ging bis an die Ufern des Schuylkill und das Lager breitete sich von Fatland Furth bis an die French

who like the Artillery were assigned in detachments *à la tête* of the brigades. The Queen's Rangers and two British battalions covered the flanks. The Jäger Corps was constantly skirmishing during the march, and camp was pitched at Valley Forge, where various magazines, a cannon foundry and a small-arms works were destroyed.

### September 21

Last night Maj. Gen. Grey[18] was detached with the light infantry, 42nd and 44th Regiments to surprise an enemy corps under General Wayne, which was said to number 1,500 men and to lie all alone in the woods. He reached the enemy at one o'clock in the morning, penetrated their left flank with unloaded muskets, killed and wounded 300, captured eighty, and took most of the baggage and many firearms. The enemy, however, had brought off the cannon. The British losses were one captain and three men killed with four wounded.

The army set off very early and marched in the following order: jägers, light infantry, Hessian Grenadiers, three Artillery Brigades, the army's baggage and train, the 4th, 2nd and 1st British Brigades. The 3rd Brigade covered the flanks and the Hessian Brigade formed the rear.

The march continued to the banks of the Schuylkill and the camp extended from Fat Land Ford to French Creek. The enemy then left their position and marched to Pottsgrove. During the march the jägers and light infantry had to skirmish as usual with the enemy when coming to defiles and woods.

Creek aus. Der Feind verliess hierauf seine Stellung und marschierte nach Potsgrove. Die Jägers und leichte Infanterie hatten während des Marsches wie gewöhnlich mit dem Feind bey vorkommenden Defileen und Wäldern zu scharmützeln.

### September 22

60 Jägers und 100 Grenadiers unter Capt. v. Wrede giengen diesen Nachmittag durch den Skuylkill über Fat Land Furth und fasten Posto, um den wahren Übergang über den Fluss zu masquieren. Die Armee setzte sich darauf des Nachts in Marsch. Lord Cornwallis commandierte die Avantgarde (die jägers *à la tête* derselben) und gieng bey Chadsfurth über den Fluss, wo die ganze Armee ohne Widerstand durchbadete. Capt. v. Wrede repassierte darauf den Fluss und kam zur Armee,

### September 23

welche sich am Morgen dergestalt lagerte, dass sich ihr linker Flügel auf dem Skuylkill stützte. Das 2e Bat. leichte Infanterie wurde nach Schwedsfurth detachiert, so vom Feind mit 6 vernagelten eisernen Canonen verlassen war.

### September 24

Alles ruhig. General Washington hatte sich gegen Skibbach Creek zurückgezogen. Wir erhielten Ordre, morgen früh mit Tages Ambruch zu marschieren.

### September 25

Die Armee marschierte in 2 Colonnen nach Germantown und bezog allda ein Lager dergestalt — Den rechten Flügel hatten die Garde und General Grands Brigade. Die Rangers und das 1ste Bat. leichte Infanterie machten das avancierte

*September 22*

Sixty jägers and one hundred grenadiers under Captain von Wreden crossed the Schuylkill this afternoon at Fat Land Ford and took post to disguise the true crossing of the river. Then at night the army began to march. Lord Cornwallis commanded the van (the jägers *à la tête*), crossing the river at Chadd's Ford, through which the entire army waded without meeting opposition. Captain von Wreden then recrossed the river and joined the army,[18]

*September 23*

which encamped in the morning with its left wing resting on the Schuylkill. The 2nd battalion light infantry was detached to Swede's Ford, which the enemy had quit, leaving behind six spiked iron cannon.

*September 24*

Everything was halted. General Washington had retired to Skippack Creek. We received orders to march at daybreak tomorrow.

*September 25*

The army marched in two columns to Germantown and camped there in the following manner. The Guards and General Grant's Brigade had the right wing. The Rangers[20] and 1st Battalion light infantry formed the advanced corps of this wing, which was supported by the Dragoons. The British infantry had the centre, in front of which lay Germantown, and the 40th Regiment and 1st Battalion light infantry[21] formed the advanced post. The Hessians

Corps dieses Flügels und die Dragoner unterstützten ihn. Das Centrum hatte die engl. Infanterie, in dessen Front lag Germantown, und das 40te Rgmt. und 1ste Bat. leichte Infanterie machten den Avant Posten. Den linken Flügel hatten die Hessen, und das Jäger Corps stand vor selbigen auf der Strasse von Lancaster nach Philadelphia. Das Grenadier Bat. von Minigroda war postiert, um die Jägers zu unterstützen. Es ist dieser Ort unter dem Namen Skylkillfall bekannt.

**September 26**

Lord Cornwallis marschierte mit denen engl. und hessischen Grenadiers um 8 Uhr diesen Morgen nach Philadelphia, das vom Feind, und vom Congress schon eine zeitlang, verlassen war. Er nahm dort Nachmittags Besitz von der Stadt und, um selbige von denen noch im Delaware liegenden feindlichen Schiffen zuschützen, liess er 3 Batterien für 6 12 lb aufwerfen, diese waren aber noch nicht fertig als

**September 27**

zwei Fregatten und verschiedene andere armierte Schiffe von Mud Island kamen und die untere Batterie mit 2 Canonen angriffen. Die grosse Fregatte von 30 Canonen *Delaware* benannt, ankerte 500 Ruthen von der Batterie, und die andere etwas weiter davon. Um 10 Uhr fingen sie an, die Stadt sowohl als auch die 3 Batterien heftig zu canonieren, da aber die Ebbe eintrat, so stiess die *Delaware* auf den Sand, worauf die 4 Canonen von derer Grenadier Bat. auf sie gerichtet wurden, welche so gute Wirkung hatten, dass sie strich und von einer Compagnie Engländer in Besitz genommen wurde. Die anderen Schiffe, nach dem die Fregatte verlohren, zogen sich zurück auf ihre vorige Station nach Mud Island.

had the left wing, and the Jäger Corps was ahead of it on the road from Lancaster to Philadelphia. The Grenadier Battalion von Minnigerode was posted to support the jägers. This place is known by the name "Falls of Schuylkill".

***September 26***

At eight o'clock this morning Lord Cornwallis marched with the British and Hessian Grenadiers to Philadelphia, which had been abandoned by the enemy, and for some time by Congress. In the afternoon he took possession of the city. To protect it from the enemy ships still lying in the Delaware, he threw up three batteries for six 12-pounders but these were not yet ready when

***September 27***

two frigates and several other armed ships came from Mud Island and attacked the lower battery of two guns. The large frigate of 30 guns, named the *Delaware*, anchored 500 rods[22] from the battery, and the other one a little farther away. At ten o'clock they began to cannonade fiercely both the city and the three batteries but because the tide ebbed, the *Delaware* ran on to the sand. The four cannon of the Grenadier Battalions were then trained on her. This had such a good effect that she struck and a company of Britishers took possession of her. After the loss of the frigate the other ships retired to their former station off Mud Island.

***September 28***

Philadelphia is well-nigh deserted by all its inhabitants. The enemy has fortified Mud Island very well. It is an island in the Delaware a few miles below Philadelphia and

*September 28*

Philadelphia ist beynahe von allen Einwohnern verlassen. Der Feind hat Mud Island sehr wohl fortificiert. Selbiges ist eine Insul, so im Delaware einige Meilen unter Philadelphia liegt und die Communication zu Wasser, die uns wegen der Provision sowohl als Überhaupt ganz unentbehrlich ist, unterbricht. Ausser denen auf dieser Insul selbst und denen Ufern des Jersey angelegten Werken hat der Feind noch eine Menge Schiffe, so zu deren Defension dienen, und selbst der Fluss ist mit *Chevaux de frise* gegen das Einlaufen unserer Schiffe verbarrikadiert. So dass wir genöthigt seyn werden, den Orth förmlich zu belagern, um uns die Communication zu eröffnen. Zu welchem Ende denn auch die nötigen Anstalten bereits gemacht werden.

*October 1*

Verwichene Nacht hatte das 10te u. 42te Rgmt. Besitz von einer Schanze genommen, so Billingsport heist und an dem Ufer des Delaware in der Jersey liegt und eigentlich die *Chevaux de frise*, so vor Mud Island im Fluss liegen, decken. Der Feind hatte keinen Widerstand gethan und die Canonen vernagelt. Unsere Schiffe fingen darauf folglich an, die unteren *Chevaux de frise* weg zu nehmen. Der Feind hingegen arbeitete sehr fleissig an Mud Island und der gegen über liegenden Schanze Redbanck.

*October 4*

Die vielen Detachements, welche der General Howe nach Philadelphia und in die Jersey geschickt, um die Stadt zu besezzen und Mud Island zu belagern, mochten den General Washington bewogen haben, besonders da er eine Verstärkung aus Virginia erhalten, die königl. Armee zu attaquieren. In dieser Absicht war er aus seinem Lager am

interrupts the communication by water, which is quite indispensable to us, both for provisions and generally. Apart from the works laid down on this island and on the banks of the Jersey, the enemy has a great many ships serving as their defence, and even the river is blocked to our ships by *chevaux de frise*.[23] And so we shall be compelled to lay siege formally to the place in order to open the communication, and already the necessary preparations are being made to this end.

## October 1

Last night the 10th and 42nd Regiments took possession of a redoubt called Billingsport. It lies on the Jersey shore of the Delaware and effectively covers the *chevaux de frise* lying in the river in front of Mud Island. The enemy had offered no opposition and had spiked the cannon. Our ships then began to remove the lower *chevaux de frise*. However, the enemy were working very diligently on Mud Island and on the redoubt opposite at Red Bank.

## October 4

The many detachments that General Howe had dispatched to Philadelphia and to Jersey to occupy the city and to besiege Mud Island may have induced General Washington to attack the royal army, especially as he had received a reinforcement from Virginia. He had set off from his camp on Skippack Creek with this intention and towards two o'clock this morning we received news of his advance. Lt. Colonel von Wurmb immediately marched out with the Jäger Corps, sent word to General Knyphausen, and occupied the bridge at Van Deering's house leading over Wissahickon Creek. Shortly afterwards we heard firing on the right wing and towards half past three the Jäger Corps

Skibbach Creek aufgebrochen und gegen 2 Uhr diesen Morgen erhielten wir die Nachricht von dessen Anmarsch. Der Oberst Lieut. v. Wurmb rückte mit dem Jägercorps sogleich aus, liess den Vorfall an den General Knyphausen melden, und besetzte die Brücke bey Van Doerens Haus, so über den Wissahickon Creek führt. Wir hörten bald darauf das Feuern am rechten Flügel und gegen ½ 4 Uhr wurde das Jäger Corps von einem Corps von 4,000 Man mit 4 6 lb attaquiert. Das Corps musste auch würklich die Brücke verlassen, setzte sich aber auf die gegen selbige liegende Höhe, und defendierte solche mit dem Büchsen Feuer gegen die wiederholten Versuche des Feindes sie zu forcieren. Die 4 feindl. Canonen spielten beständig auf die Jägers, ohne dass unsere 3 lb den Feind erreichen konnten. Das Feuer wurde inzwischen algemein und sehr heftig auf dem rechten Flügel, bis gegen 9 Uhr der General Lieutnant v. Knyphausen sagen liess, dass der feindl. linke Flügel geschlagen sey. Hierauf attaquierte der Oberstlieut. v. Wurmb die Brücke aufs neue und vertrieb den Feind sowohl von da als auch der gegen überliegenden Höhe unter einem heftigen Feuer. Da die Attaque durch eine langes Defilee geschehen musste, so hatte man feindl. Seits Zeit sich zu retirieren. Wir fanden dahero auch nur 20 Todte, und da die Jägers ohnehin schon sehr fatiguiert und nicht unterstützt wurden, auch nur in 300 Man bestanden, so geschah keine weitere Verfolgung.

Im Centro der Armee war der Feind auf die leichte Infanterie gefallen und hatte solche zurück geschlagen. Der Oberstlieut. Musgrave warf sich aber mit dem 40ten Rgmt. in ein steinernes Haus, welches vom Feinde angegriffen wurde und wo er sich bey aufhielt, sonst hätte er viel geschwinder und noch ehe einmal die Armee alle im Gewehr gewesen, solche attaquieren können. So aber attaquierte die Armee ihn, schlug ihn aus der Stadt hinaus und in die Flucht. Er retirierte sich hierauf in sein voriges

was attacked by a corps of 4,000 men with four 6-pounders. The Corps had in fact to abandon the bridge but occupied the height opposite, defending it with rifle fire against the repeated attempts of the enemy to force it. The four enemy cannon were constantly playing upon the jägers without our 3-pounders being able to reach the enemy. Meanwhile the firing became general and very heavy on the right wing until Lt. Gen. von Knyphausen sent word towards nine o'clock that the enemy left wing was beaten. Lt. Colonel von Wurmb then attacked the bridge afresh and dislodged the enemy both from there and from the height opposite under a heavy fire. As the attack had to take place through a long defile, those on the enemy side had time to retire. Consequently we found only twenty dead. No further pursuit took place, for, as things stood, the jägers were already very tired, were not supported, and consisted only of 300 men.

In the centre of the army the enemy had fallen upon the light infantry and driven them back. However, Lt. Colonel Musgrave[24] threw himself with the 40th Regiment into a stone house, which was attacked by the enemy, who were held up there. Otherwise they would have been able to attack the army much more speedily and before all of it had been under arms. As it was, the army attacked them, drove them from the town, and put them to flight. They then retired to their former camp on Skippack Creek, leaving behind 300 dead, 600 wounded, and 400 prisoners. Our own losses are 400 dead and wounded. General Agnew[25] is among the former.

Lord Cornwallis, who heard the firing in Philadelphia, immediately marched off three Grenadier Battalions from there. He himself arrived soon enough to take part in the last action but the battalions came too late.

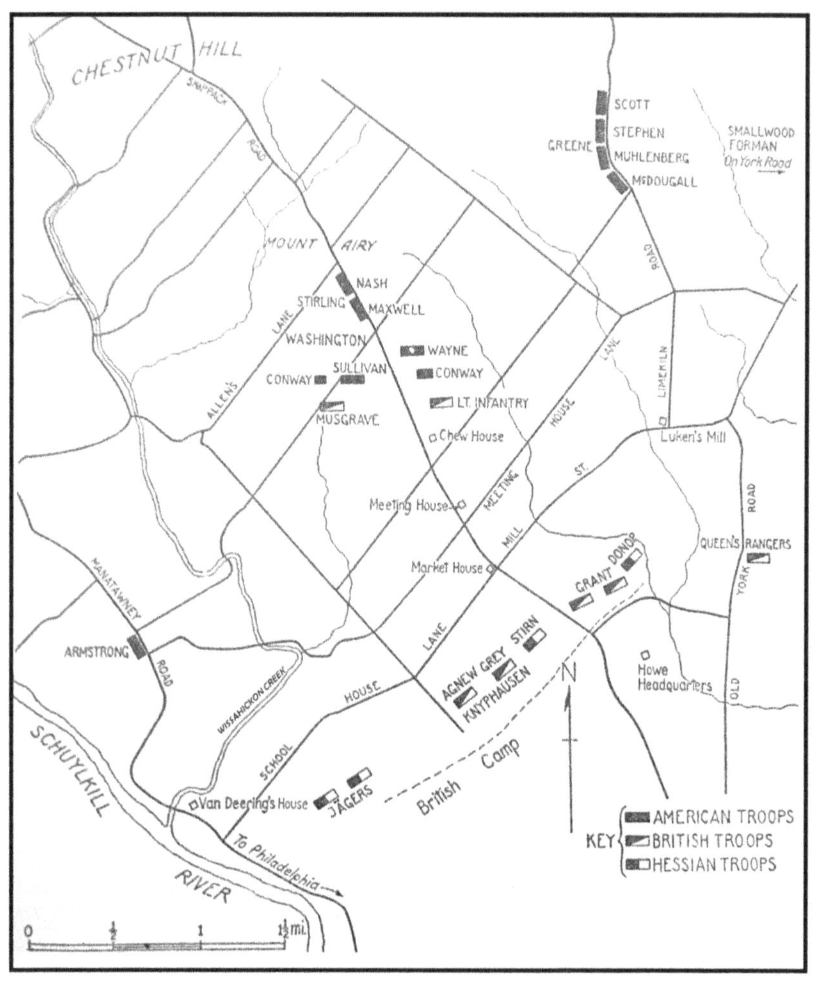



**The Battle of Germantown**
**4 October 1777**

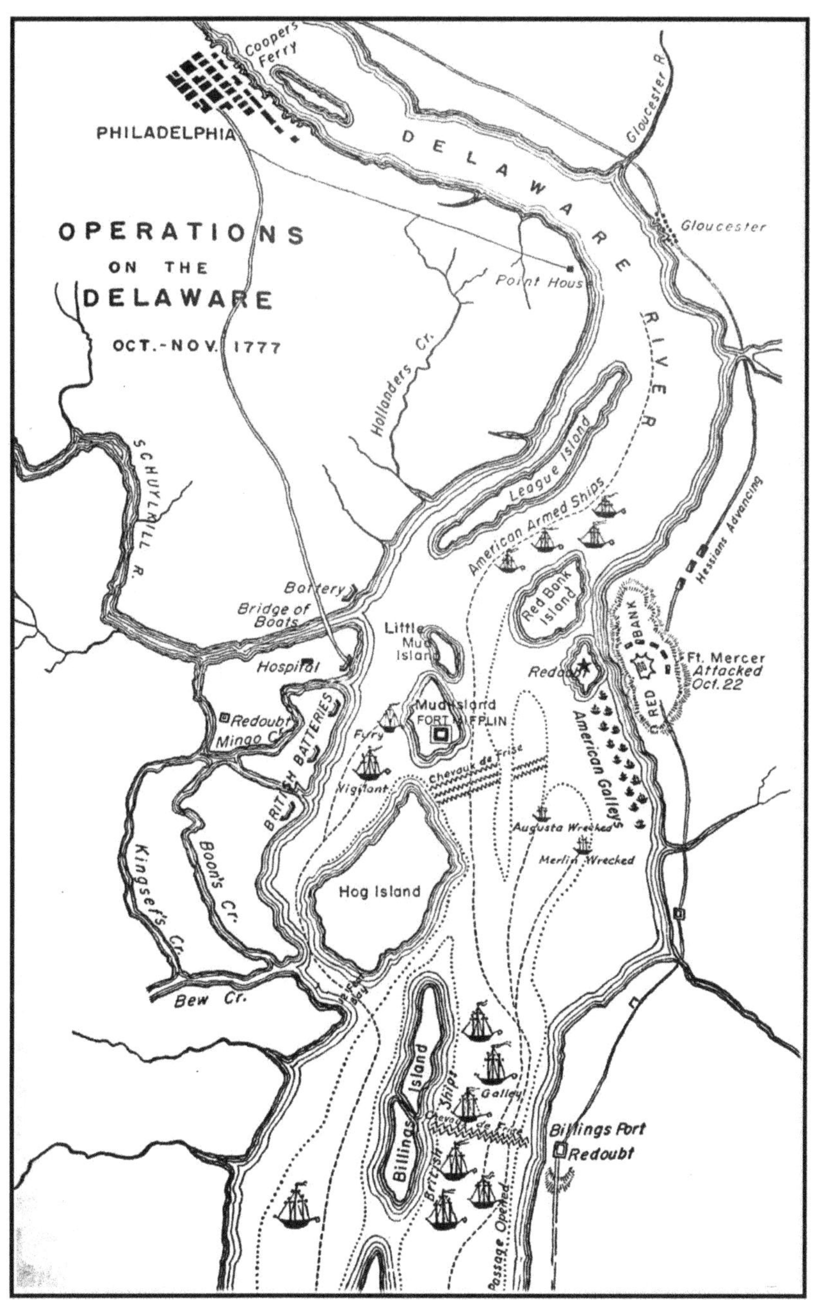

Coopers Ferry
PHILADELPHIA
DELAWARE
Gloucester R.
Gloucester
OPERATIONS
ON THE
DELAWARE
OCT.-NOV. 1777
Point Hous
Hollanders Cr.
League Island
DELAWARE RIVER
SCHUYLKILL R.
American Armed Ships
Hessians Advancing
Battery
Bridge of Boats
Little Mud Island
Red Bank Island
RED BANK
Ft. Mercer Attacked Oct. 22
Hospital
Redoubt
Redoubt Mingo Cr.
Mud Island FORT MIFFLIN
Ferry
American Galleys
BRITISH BATTERIES
Vigilant
Chevaux de Frise
Augusta Wrecked
Merlin Wrecked
Kingsef's Cr.
Boon's Cr.
Hog Island
Bew Cr.
Billings Island
Ships
Galley
British
Chevaux de Frise
Billings Port
Redoubt
Passage Opened

Lager an der Skibbach Creek unter Zurücklassung von 300 Todten, 600 blessierten und 400 Gefangenen. Der unsrige Verlust is gliechwohl 400 Todte und blessierte. Unter ersteren befand sich der General Agnew.

Lord Cornwallis, welcher das Feuer in Philadelphia gehört hatte, setzte sogleich von da 3 Grenadier Bataillons in Marsch. Er für seine Person kam auch zeitig genug, um an der letzten Action Theil zu nehmen. Die Bataillons aber kamen zu spat.

## October 5

Gestern war unsere Flotte von der Cheassapeak in dem Delaware ohnweit Newcastle angekommen und wird nunmehro mit allem Fleiss an der Eroberung von Mud Island arbeiten, um endlich die Communication zu eröffnen, um da durch wenigstens die Zufuhr der Provision zu erleichtern, den gegenwärtig bringen nur kleine Boote das nöthigste, welche sich des Nachts durch die feindl. Schiffe durch stehlen müssen.

## October 6

Die feindl. Werke zu Mud Island bestehen in einem Forth mit 4 Block Häusern, zwey schwimmenden Batterien, jede von 9 Canonen, 14 Galeeren mit schweren Canonen, und viele andere armierte Fahrzeuge. Gerade gegenüber auf der Jersey liegt Redbanck, so die Schiffe deckt, und vor denen Werken liegen *Chevaux de frise,* so den Eingang deren Schiffe versperrend.

Nachrichten von New York sagen folgendes:

> Den 22 Aug. wagte der Feind unter Gen. Maj. Schmalwood eine Landung auf Staatenisland und überrumpelte 2 Rgmt. Provincialen, welche die Vorposten hatten und

*October 5*

Yesterday our fleet from the Chesapeake arrived in the Delaware off Newcastle. It will now work extremely hard on the capture of Mud Island in order to open the communication at last, thereby facilitating at least the conveyance of provisions, for at present there are just small boats bringing only the most needed supplies, and they have to steal past the enemy ships at night.

*October 6*

The enemy works at Mud Island consist of a fort with four block houses, two floating batteries, each of nine guns, fourteen galleys with heavy guns, and many other armed vessels. Directly opposite in Jersey is Red Bank covering the ships, and in front of the works are *chevaux de frise* blocking the entry of the ships.

There are reports from New York of the following:

On 22 August the enemy under Maj. Gen. Smallwood[26] ventured a landing on Staten Island and surprised two regiments of Provincials holding the outposts, who were not on their guard. On hearing the din, the British troops under Brig. Gen. Campbell[27] marched out in pursuit of the enemy, overtook them at one o'clock, and engaged them just as they were about to retire into the boats. About 300 men fell into the hands of the British.

On 12 September General Clinton went with part of the troops from York Island to Jersey to amuse the enemy and to make a diversion in favour of both General Howe and General Burgoyne. The militia offered the General some

nicht auf ihrer Huth waren. Auf diesen Lärmen rückten die englischen Trouppen unter Br. Gen. Campbel aus und setzten dem Feinde nach, holten ihn um 1 Uhr ein und engagierten solchen just da er sich in die Boote retirieren wollte. Es fielen gegen 300 Mann in engl. Hände.

12 Sept. ging General Clinton mit einem Theil derer Trouppen von Yorkisland in die Jersey, um den Feind zu amusieren und *en faveur* des Gen. Howe sowohl als Gen. Burgoyne eine Diversion zu machen. Die Miliz that dem General einigen Widerstand. Er hielt sich bis 16 Sept. auf und hatte während dieser Zeit viel Vieh zum Behütte derer Hospitaler eintreiben lassen.

27 Sept. war eine Flotte mit Provisionen und Recroutten zu New York angekommen, wobey denn auch die zwey neuen Jäger Compagnien v. Wurmb und Lorey befindlich sind. General Clinton machte dahero gleich Anstalten, dem General Burgoyne auf dem Nord River entgegen zu gehen.

*October 19*

Die Armee brach heute von Germantown auf und marschierte nach Philadelphia, alwo solche auf denen Höhen vor der Stadt bey Morris House ein Lager bezogen, um näher zu seyn, die Operationen gegen Mud Island zu unterstützen.

*October 21*

Der Oberst von Donop mit dem Jäger Corps, der Grenadier Brigade und dem Rgmt. von Mirbach ging heute über den Delaware bey Philadelphia und landete bey Coopers Ferry, um das Forth RedBanck weg zunehmen. Er marschierte gegen Haddonfield und fasste allda gegen Abends Posto.

opposition. He stayed till 16 September and during this time drove in a lot of cattle for the benefit of the hospitals.

On 27 September a fleet arrived at New York with provisions and recruits, including the two new jäger companies von Wurmb and Lorey. General Clinton therefore made immediate preparations to go up the North River towards General Burgoyne.

## October 19

Today the army set off from Germantown and marched to Philadelphia, where it moved into camp on the heights before the city at Morris House in order to be nearer to support the operations against Mud Island.

## October 21

Today Colonel von Donop crossed the Delaware at Philadelphia with the Jäger Corps, the Grenadier Brigade, and the Regiment von Mirbach, landing at Cooper's Ferry to take the fort at Red Bank. He marched towards Haddonfield and took post there towards evening.

## October 22

These troops set off towards four o'clock in the morning, marching via Strawberry Bank towards the fort at Red Bank, where they arrived towards midday at a distance of a quarter of a mile. The enemy had been informed of the approach of these troops this morning and were working hard to prepare their defence. The fort was immediately summoned, and as Colonel Greene,[28] the officer commanding there, was not prepared to surrender, preparations were made for storming it. The assault began

*October 22*

Gegen 4 Uhr des Morgens brachen diese Trouppen auf, marschierten über Strawberrybank gegen das Forth Redbanck, allwo sie gegen Mittag und zwar in der Entfernung von ¼ Meilen ankamen. Der Feind war von dem Anmarsch dieser Trouppen diesen Morgen benachrichtigt worden und arbeitete sehr, um sich zu defendieren. Das Forth wurde sofort aufgefordert und da der commandierende Offr. Oberst Green sich nicht ergeben wollte, wurden Anstalten zum Sturm gemacht, welcher gegen 4 Uhr des Nachmittags seinen Anfang nahm und bis in die Abend Dämmerung dauerte, aber zum desswillen unglücklich ausfiel, weilen der Wall zu hoch und keine Sturmleitern da waren. Das Jäger Corps deckte beyde Flanquen gegen das Wasser, um eine allenfalsige Landung von denen Schiffen zu verhindern, welche aber demohngeachtet durch ihre Cannonade sehr viel Schaden tathen. Der Oberst von Donop wurde am Rande des Grabens tödlich blessiert und wollte deswegen nicht zurückgebracht seyn, gerieth dahero auch in feindliche Hände. Die Trouppen, nachdem sie unter einem heftigen Feuer bis in den Graben hervor gedrungen waren und das Werk zu ersteigen unpracticable war, zogen sich darauf zurück. Das Jäger Corps machte die Arrière bis auf eine gewisse Distance. Nachher machte die Hälfte davon die Avantgarde, um die Brücke über den Timber Creek zu gewinnen, indem zu befürchten, dass solche vom Feind besetzt seyn könne. Der Feind hielt sich im Forth ganz ruhig und das ganze Corps lagerte sich jenseits Timber Creek, retournierte über

*October 23*

Haddonfield und repassierte den Delaware noch denselben Tag und kam im Lager der Armee wieder an. Den Angriff auf das Forth hätten einige Kriegsschiffe begünstigen

towards four o'clock and lasted till dusk, but the outcome was unfortunate, for the rampart was too high and there were no scaling ladders there. The Jäger Corps covered both flanks towards the water to prevent any landing from the ships, which nonetheless did a great deal of damage with their cannonading. Colonel von Donop was mortally wounded at the edge of the ditch and therefore did not wish to be brought back. So he fell into the hands of the enemy. After they had pressed forward into the ditch under a heavy fire and found that scaling the work was impracticable, the troops withdrew. For some distance the Jäger Corps formed the rear. Afterwards half of it formed the van to gain the bridge over Timber Creek for fear that it might have been occupied by the enemy. The enemy kept quite inactive in the fort and the whole corps camped on the other side of Timber Creek. It returned

*October 23*

via Haddonfield, recrossing the Delaware the same day, and arrived again in the camp of the army. Some warships should have supported the attack on the fort, but owing to the contrary wind they were unable to come up. On the next day, the 23rd, they did do so — the *Augusta* of 64 guns and two frigates — but they ran on to the *chevaux de frise* and had to be set on fire.

After the failure of this affair batteries were thrown up with the greatest difficulty on the marshes of Province Island, but they did not begin to play until 10 November and, to be candid, had very little effect.

*November 15*

The wind was good today, and particularly as there was a spring tide (when the water is one or more feet higher,

sollen, wegen des widrigen Windes aber konnten solche nicht herauf kommen. Den anderen Tag aber, nämlich den 23ten, kamen sie — die *Augusta* von 64 Canonen nebst 2 Fregatten, kamen aber auf die *Chevaux de frise* und mussten angesteckt werden.

Nach dieser mislungenen Affaire wurden mit den grössten Beschwerlichkeiten Batterien in denen Morästen zu Provinz Island aufgeworfen, welche allererst

*November 10*

zu spielen anfingen und im Grunde sehr wenig Effect hatten.

*November 15*

Der Wind war heute gut, und besonders weilen es Spring Tide war (wo das Wasser um 1 und mehr Schuh höher ist und dies geschieht nur bey jeder Monds Veränderung), konnte man die Schiffe gegen Mud Island gebrauchen. Der *Vigilant*, ein 24 Canonen Schiff mit 16 24 lb, segelte mit einer Schaluppe von 3 24 lb unterm Lieuthenant Hotham durch den Canal zwischen Provinz und Hog Island gegen das Forth. Es gab eine heftige Canonade, welche dem Feind viel Schaden that und

*November 16*

ihn nöthigte das Forth und die Insul in der Nacht zu abandonieren, ihre Schiffe in Brand zu stecken u. sich in die Jersey zu retirieren, und wäre solches nicht geschehen, so war die englische Garde schon beordert solches zu stürmen. Die englischen Grenadiers nahmen dahero solches in Besitz und man behauptet, dass sich der

which occurs only at every changing of the moon), it was possible to bring the ships against Mud Island, The *Vigilant*, a 24-gun ship with sixteen 24-pounders, and a sloop of three 24-pounders under Lieutenant Hotham[29] sailed against the fort through the channel between Province and Hog Islands. There was a heavy cannonade, which did the enemy a lot of damage,

## November 16

forcing them at night to abandon the fort and the island, to set fire to their ships, and to retire to Jersey. Had this not occurred, the British Guards were already under orders to storm the fort. The British Grenadiers therefore took possession of it, and it is said that the enemy losses during the siege amount to 400 dead and wounded. The royal losses are seven dead and five wounded.

## November 17

Yesterday a fleet arrived in the Delaware off Chester. General Clinton had sent it to General Howe with troop reinforcements after General Burgoyne's army had been captured and his expedition up the North River had been in vain.

The news of that misfortune is as follows:

> As soon as the fleet from England had arrived at New York on 27 September, General Clinton went up the North River on 1 October, and on the 6th he took Forts Montgomery and Clinton, which lie on either bank of the river. This happened by storming them towards six o'clock in the evening. The Regiment von Trumbach and the two newly arrived jäger companies from Germany were present

feindliche Verlust auf 400 Todte und blessierte während der Belagerung belaufen. Der königl. ist 7 Todte und 5 blessierte.

*November 17*

Gestern war eine Flotte bey Chester in dem Delaware angekommen, welche der General Clinton, nachdem die Armee des General Burgoyne gefangen und dessen den Nord River hinaufgemachte Expedition vergebens gewesen, an den General Howe mit einer Verstärkung von Trouppen geschickt.

Die Nachrichten von jenem Unglück sind folgende:

Sobald die Flotte von England den 27 Sept. in Newyork angekommen war, ging General Clinton den 1 October den Nord River hinauf und nahm 6ten dato die Forths Montgomery und Clinton, welche an beyden Unfern des Flusses liegen. Dies geschah des Nachmittags gegen 6 Uhr mit stürmender Hand. Das Rgmt. von Trumbach und die 2 neuerdings aus Teutschland angekommenen Jäger Compagnien waren bey diesem Vorfall zu gegen. Nachdem die Werke beyderseitig genommen, steckte der Feind seyne beyden Fregatten *Montgomery* and *Congress* in Brand und einige andere Schiffe retirierten sich den Fluss hinauf. Das Forth Constitution, so noch etwas weiter am Fluss hinauf lag, wurde hierauf aufgefordert, und da sich solches nicht ergeben wollte, wurde am 7 October ein Detachement abgeschickt, um solches zu stürmen, bey seiner Annäherung aber hatte es der Feind schon verlassen. Mehr als 100 Canonen und eine Menge Kriegsbedürfnisse wurden dem Feind bey diesen Gelegenheiten abgenommen.

Der General Vaughan ging mit einem Detachement und Sir James Wallace mit denen Schiffen den Fluss hinauf,

during these proceedings. After the works on either side had been taken, the enemy set fire to both their frigates, *Montgomery* and *Congress*, whilst some other ships retired up river. Fort Constitution, lying a little farther up river, was then summoned. As it refused to surrender, a detachment was dispatched on 7 October to storm it, but the enemy had already abandoned it on their approach. More than one hundred cannon and a great quantity of war material were taken from the enemy during these proceedings.

General Vaughan[30] went up river with a detachment, and Sir James Wallace[31] with the ships. On 15 October they landed at Esopus, where part of the enemy were entrenched, attacked them, and took most of them prisoner. They went on to burn the town. Then this corps went still farther up river with the intention of opening the communication with General Burgoyne and joining him, but unfortunately the entire project was frustrated by news that the General had surrendered at Saratoga on 16 October as a prisoner of war. As soon as the troops were convinced of the truth of this disaster, they returned to Montgomery, which was razed to the ground and abandoned at once. The troops had already arrived back in New York on 24 October, they were immediately taken on board the ships, and they reached the Delaware on 9 November.

## November 18

This night Lord Cornwallis marched out of the camp at Philadelphia with fifty jägers (Captain von Wreden), a battalion of light infantry, a British battalion of grenadiers, the Grenadier Battalion von Lengerke, and the 33rd Regiment. He crossed the Delaware at Chester on the 19th, joining up with the troops who had arrived from New York

landeten d. 15 Oct. zu Esopus, wo sich ein Theil des Feindes verschanzt hatte, griffen solchen an, machten den grössten Theil gefangen und verbrannten darauf die Stadt. Hiernächst ging dieses Corps noch immer weiter den Fluss hinauf, in der Absicht mit dem General Burgoyne die Communication zu eröffnen und ihm entgegen zu gehen. Unglücklicherweise aber wurde durch die Nachricht, dass sich dieser General am 16ten October zu Saratoga zum Kriegs-gefangenen ergeben habe, das ganze Project vereitelt, und die Trouppen, sobald sie von der Wahrheit dieses Unglücks überzeugt waren, retournierten nach Montgomery, welcher Ort denn auch geschleift und sogleich verlassen wurde. Die Trouppen kamen bereits den 24ten October zu Newyork wieder an und wurden sogleich auf die Schiffe gebracht und erreichten den Delaware den 9ten November.

*November 18*

Lord Cornwallis marschierte diese Nacht mit 50 Jägers (Capt. von Wrede), einem Bat. leichte Infanterie, einem englischen und dem Grenadier Bat. von Lengercke, nebst dem 33ten Rgmt., aus dem Lager bey Philadelphia, passierte den 19. den Delaware bey Chester und conjugierte sich mit denen zu Billingsport bereits gelandeten, von Newyork unterm General Major Wilson angekommenen, Trouppen.

*November 21*

Lord Cornwallis setzte sich mit obigem Corps in den Marsch, um das Forth Redbanck weg zunehmen, welches der Feind, nachdem er Mud Island verlohren, noch im Besitze hatte und unter dessen Canonen sich die fiendl. Schiffe retiriert hatten. Der Lord marschierte über Mende

under Maj. Gen. Wilson[32] and who had already landed at Billingsport.

*November 21*

Lord Cornwallis marched off with the above corps to take the fort at Red Bank. After losing Mud Island, the enemy still possessed Red Bank, and under its guns the enemy ships had retired. His Lordship marched across Manto Bridge and camped at Woodbury, where he received news that the enemy had abandoned the fort and had set fire to all their ships. The general then detached the British Grenadiers to take possession of the fort.

*November 24*

This corps marched to the vicinity of the fort at Red Bank.

*November 25*

Today the march was to Gloucester, from where the corps was to recross the Delaware and rejoin the army. While the necessary preparations for this were being made, the jäger detachment under Captain von Wreden was posted to cover the crossing. Towards four o'clock in the afternoon an enemy corps under General Greene,[33] coming from Mount Holly, attacked this post and was repulsed, but only after a very fierce action in which both parties alternately retired till, with night falling, the enemy withdrew. The losses of the jägers were one officer and four men dead, one officer and thirteen men wounded, and ten men missing. The enemy losses could not be determined, for, apart from one dead officer, they took their dead and wounded with them.

Bridge und lagerte sich bey Woodburry, wo er die Nachricht erhielt, dass der Feind das Forth verlassen und alle seine Schiffe angesteckt habe. Hierauf detachierte der General die engl. Grenadiers, um das Forth in Besitz zu nehmen.

*November 24*

Marschierte dieses Corps bis in die Gegend des Forths Redbanck.

*November 25*

Der Marsch war heute bis Gloucester, von welchem Ort das Corps den Delaware repassieren und wieder zur Armee stossen sollte. Während denn dazu die nöthigen Anstalten gemacht wurden, war das Detachement derer Jägers unter dem Capitaine von Wrede so postiert, dass solches den Übergang decken sollte. Gegen 4 Uhr des Nachmittags attaquierte ein feindliches Corps unterm General Green, so von Mountholly herkam, diesen Posten, wurde aber repoussiert und zwar nach einem hizzigen Gefechte, wo beyde Partheyen wechselweise retirierten bis mit einbrechender Nacht der Feind sich zurück zog. Der Verlust der Jägers war 1 Offr, 4 M. todt, 1 Offr, 13 M. blessiert und 10 M. vermisst. Der feindliche war nicht zu bestimmen, indem er seine Todten and blessierten, ausser einem todten Officier, mit sich weg nahm.

*November 26*

Repassierte das ganze Corps den Delaware, wurde nur durch einige Feinde verfolgt, und vereiningte sich sodann mit der Armee im Lager bey Philadelphia. Mithin war nunmehro und endlich die Communication des Delaware

*November 26*

The whole corps recrossed the Delaware, pursued by only a few of the enemy, and joined the army in camp at Philadelphia. Thus was now opened at last the communication along the Delaware. It had cost a lot of time and trouble and many lives.

The enemy losses are reckoned to be —

> as respects Mud Island, one 32-pounder, one 24-pounder, seven 18-pounders, and one 12-pounder,

> as respects the fort at Red Bank, six 18-pounders, three 12-pounders, two 6-pounders, and five 4-pounders,

> and between 3 and 400 dead and wounded.

During all the operations on the Delaware General Washington kept particularly inactive in his camp at Whitemarsh near Germantown. He had meanwhile fortified it to some extent with an abatis and some redoubts, drawing a reinforcement from the northern army.

*December 4*

At eleven o'clock this night the army marched in two columns towards Germantown. As it was night-time and dark, the light infantry formed the van and the jägers followed. The enemy advanced posts constantly skirmished with us during the advance and at daybreak the army reached Chestnut Hill, drawing up in front of the enemy right wing. The Jäger Corps was assigned its post in front of the left wing, and on its right, about in the centre of the army, was posted the light infantry, also advanced.

eröffnet, welche viel Zeit und Mühe und viele Menschen gekostet hatte.

Man rechnet die feindl. Verluste —

1 32 lb, 1 24 lb, 7 18 lb, 1 12 lb für Mud Island,

6 18 lb, 3 12 lb, 2 6 lb, 5 4 lb für Forth Redbanck,

und zwischen 3 und 400 Todte und blessierte.

General Washington hielt sich während allen denen Operationen in der Delaware besonders ruhig in seinem Lager zu White Marsh ohnweit German Town, welches er in zwischen einigermassen durch einen Verhack und einige Redutten befestigen liess und hatte eine Verstärkung von der nordlichen Armee an sich gezogen.

## *December 4*

Die Armee marschierte diese Nacht um 11 Uhr gegen Germantown in 2 Colonnen und weilen es nacht und dunkel war, machte die Light Infantry die Avantgarde, auf welche die Jägers folgten. Die feindl. avancierten Posten haranguierten beständig während dem Vorrücken und mit Tages Anbruch erreichte die Armee Chestnutshill und marschierte in Front des feindl. rechten Flügels auf. Das Jäger Corps bekam seinen Posten vor dem linken Flügel und ihm zur rechten ohngefähr in Centro der Armee standt die leichte Infanterie, ebenwohl avanciert. Gegen 9 Uhr setzte sich ein Corps von ohngefähr 300 Mann vom feindl. rechten Flügel in Bewegung und postierte sich auf einer dem Jäger Corps gegenüber gelegenen Höhe, so dass die Posten nacheinender schossen. Gegen 11 Uhr detachierte der Feind ein anderes Corps von ohngefähr 1,000 Mann,

Towards nine o'clock a corps of some 300 men from the enemy right wing was put in motion and took post on a height opposite the Jäger Corps, so that both parties were firing at each other.  Towards eleven o'clock the enemy detached another corps of some 1,000 men, who attacked the light infantry posted in front of the centre but were repulsed after a short engagement in which the enemy lost many men.  Many including the commander of the corps were captured.

*December 6*

The corps posted in front of the Jäger Corps pulled back this night without having attempted anything, except that the patrols had been firing here and there and as a result we had three wounded. The two armies stood within sight of each other. The enemy's, which was on a height, was covered by some redoubts and abatis. Washington appeared to expect an attack and altered none of his dispositions, but General Howe thought the enemy's position here too strong and therefore wanted to attempt their left wing. So the army abandoned its position

*December 7*

and marched off to the right towards Abingdon Township against the enemy's left flank, where it arrived in the afternoon, drawing up in front of it. An enemy advanced corps had to be dislodged before the army could encamp, so the Jäger Corps was ordered to do the job.

We found the enemy posted very advantageously on a steep height.  The Jäger Corps marched on in line and drove them back slmost to their abatis. They were a corps of so-called riflemen who had recently joined General

welches die leichte Infanterie, so vor dem Centro postiert war, angriff, aber nach einem kurzen Gefecht zurück geschlagen wurde. Der Feind verlohr hierbey viele Leuthe und viele, samt dem Commandeur des Corps, wurden gefangen.

*December 6*

Das vor dem Jäger Corps postiert gewesene Corps zog sich diese Nacht wieder zurück, ohne etwas unternommen zu haben, ausser dass die Patrouillen herumschossen, wodurch wir 3 blessierte erhielten. Die beyden Armeen standen sich einender im Gesicht, die feindl. auf einer Höhe und wurde durch einige Redutten und Verhacks gedeckt. Washington schien einen Angriff zu erwarten und änderte nichts an seiner Stellung. General Howe aber glaubte die feindl. Position hier zu stark und wollte also dessen linken Flügel versuchen. Die Armee verliess dahero ihre Stellung

*December 7*

und marschierte rechts ab nach Abingdon Township gegen die feindl. linke Flanque, woselbst sie des Nachmittags ankam und in deren Front aufmarschierte. Ein feindliches avanciertes Corps war nöthig zu delogieren ehe die Armee das Lager beziehen konnte, das Jäger Corps wurde dahero beordert dieses zu thun.

Wir fanden den Feind auf einer steilen Höhe sehr vortheilhaft postiert. Das Jäger Corps marschierte *en front* heran und schlug ihn bis beynahe in ihren Verhau zurück. Es war ein Corps sogenannter Riflemen, so kürzlich von Canada zu des Gen. Washingtons Armee gestossen waren, und bestanden in ohngefähr 500 Mann. Da unsere Cavallerie sich mit der feindl. abgeben musste, so machten

Washington's army from Canada and consisted of about 500 men. Because our cavalry was necessarily occupied with the enemy's, we took only thirty prisoners and we ourselves had three dead and nine wounded, whilst the enemy had about thirty dead. After this affair had ended, the army encamped. The Jäger Corps came to lie very near to the enemy's outposts, so the pickets were constantly firing at each other.

### December 8

Today, quite contrary to all expectations, the army marched back to Philadelphia, for the general found the enemy position too strong to attack. Marching off took place in complete silence. The jägers formed the rear and all that could be seen of the enemy were a few cavalrymen.

### December 10

Lord Cornwallis crossed the Schuylkill with 3,600 men to gather forage. The van of this corps, consisting of a detachment of mounted and foot jägers (Captain Cramon) and light infantry, encountered an enemy party and either captured or completely dispersed it. His Lordship marched to Swede's Ford, where he came upon the enemy on the other side of the Schuylkill on the march to encamp at Valley Forge. The enemy believed that the royal army intended to attack them and drew up in order of battle. Lord Cornwallis kept them amused the whole day through, but

### December 11

returned to Philadelphia, for he had achieved his aims so far as the forage was concerned. In fact he was not troubled once during his retreat.

wir nur 30 Gefangene und wir selbst hatten 3 Todte und 9 blessierte, der Feind aber gegen 30 Todte. Nach dem diese Affaire geendigt, bezog die Armee ein Lager. Das Jäger Corps kam sehr nahe an die feindl. Posten zu stehen, weswegen die Piquets beständig auf einander feuerten.

*December 8*

Ganz gegen alle Erwartung marschierte die Armee heute nach Philadelphia zurück, weilen der General die feindliche Position für einen Angriff zu stark fand. Der Abmarsch geschah ganz in der Stille. Die Jägers machten die Arrière und der Feind liess sich nur durch einige Cavalleristen observieren.

*December 10*

Lord Cornwallis ging mit 3,600 Mann über den Schuylkill, um Fourage ein zusammeln. Die Avantgarde dieses Corps, bestehend aus einem Detachement Jägers (Capt. Cramon) zu Pferde und zu Fuss und leichter Infanterie, waren auf eine feindliche Parthey gestossen und hatten solche Theils gefangen oder aber gänzlich zerstreuet. Der Lord rückte bis Swedesfurth, wo er den Feind jenseits des Schuylkill im Marsch antraff, um ein Lager zu Valley Forge zu beziehen. Der Feind glaubte die königl. Armee wollte ihn attaquieren und rangierte sich in *Ordre de Bataille*. My Lord Cornwallis amüsierte ihn auch den ganzen Tag über, ging aber

*December 11*

nach Philadelphia zurück, indem er seine Absichten die Fourage betreffend insoweit erreicht hatte. Er wurde auch in seiner Retraite nicht einmal beunruhigt.

*December 13*

According to reports, General Washington has indeed moved his camp to Valley Forge and is having huts built to winter there.

*December 22*

General Howe crossed the Schuylkill with the entire army, extending its left wing beyond Derby, merely for the purpose of foraging.  Meanwhile the enemy army kept quite inactive, except that the light troops were almost constantly skirmishing with each other.  The jägers formed the advanced post in front of the right wing and had several wounded.

*December 27*

A deep snow fell, completely covering the army, for it was camping without tents or huts.

*December 29*

The army marched back into the old camp at Philadelphia. The jägers formed the rear and were pursued by a party, but it did no great harm.

*December 30*

The army moved into winter quarters in the city of Philadelphia.  The jägers were quartered on the so-called Philadelphia Neck, which is the spit of land between the Delaware and the Schuylkill.  To our great surprise and quite contrary to all expectations the winter quarters were

*December 13*

Nachrichten zu Folge hat General Washington sein Lager zu Valley Forge würklich genommen und lässt Hütten bauen, um daselbst zu überwintern.

*December 22*

General Howe ging mit der gantzen Armee über den Schuylkill und extendierte deren linken Flügel bis jenseits Derby, bloss in der Absicht zu fouragieren. Die feindl. Armee verhielt sich dabey ganz ruhig, nur dass die leichten Trouppen fast für beständig zusammen haranguierten. Die Jägers hatten den Vorposten vor dem rechten Flügel und verschiedene blessierte.

*December 27*

Fiel ein tiefer Schnee, wodurch die Armee ganz zugeschneit wurde, indem solche ohne Zelter und Hütten campierte.

*December 29*

Marschierte die Armee in das alte Lager bey Philadelphia zurück. Die Jägers machten die Arrière und wurden von einer Parthey verfolgt, die aber keinen grossen Schaden that.

*December 30*

Bezog die Armee die Winter Quartiere in der Stadt Philadelphia. Die Jägers wurden im sogenannten Philadelphia Neck einquartiert, welches die Erdspitze zwischen dem Delaware und Schuylkill ist. Die Winter Quartiere, ohngeachtet die Armeen nicht weit von einander entfernt waren, besonders aber weilen jederman dafür hielt,

very peaceful, although the armies were not far apart and everyone thought in particular that the enemy's camp was very exposed. The royal army had very comfortable quarters and was covered by eleven redoubts that formed a chain from the Delaware to the Schuylkill across Morris Height. Each of these redoubts was occupied by a captain and fifty men, who were relieved every twenty-four hours. On the banks of the Schuylkill were posted pickets of Provincial troops, and the Jäger Corps had two on the Delaware at the so-called Holland Ferry and Greenwich Point.

The enemy remain at Valley Forge and have built huts in which they are wintering. The deserters who come in frequently and all reports agree that the army is in the most miserable circumstances; that it particularly lacks appointments, salt and spirituous liquors; and that the denial of these necessaries is causing nasty illnesses. Our army, on the other hand, has everything it needs, is in good health, and although the enemy are making every effort to cut off the supply of fresh food, this is causing no shortage but an extraordinary rise in its price.

dass das feindliche Lager sich sehr exponiert habe, waren ganz gegen aller Erwartung und zu unser nicht geringen Verwunderung sehr ruhig. Die königl. Armee hatte sehr bequeme Quartiere und wurde durch 11 Redutten, so eine Kette vom Delaware bis zum Schuylkill über die Morris Höhe formierten, gedeckt. Diese Redutten besetzten jede ein Capitaine mit 50 Mann, so alle 24 Stunden abgelöst wurden. An den Ufern des Schuylkill waren Piquets von Provincial Trouppen postiert und das Jäger Corps hatte deren 2 am Delaware an der sogenannten Holland Ferry und Greenwich Point.

Der Feind stehet an der Valley Forge und hat sich Hütten erbauet, worin er überwintert. Die einkommenden häufigen Deserteurs und alle Nachrichten kommen darinnen überein, dass sich die Armee in den elendsten Umständen befände, dass es ihnen besonders an Montierungsstücken, Salz und Spirituosen Getränken fehle, und dass diese ihnen abgehenden Nothwendigkeiten böse Krankheiten nach sich zögen. Die unsrige Armee hat hingegen alles was ihr nöthig thut, ist gesund, und obleich der Feind sich alle Mühe gibt, uns die frischen Lebens Mittel abzuschneiden, so verursacht dieses dennoch keinen Mangel daran, wohl aber eine ausser ordentliche Theuerung derselben.

# ∞ 1778 ∞

*Merz 12*

Ein kleines Detachement Engländer ging auf ein Fouragier Commando an beyden Ufern des Delaware hinab und brachte eine Quantität Heu ein, ohne dass ihnen das geringste begegnet wäre. Verschiedene streifende Partheyen wurden von Philadelphia zwar aus geschickt, allein selbige bestehen aus rohen, neu errichteten Provincialen, welche nur auf Rechnung der Armee plündern und sich nie mit dem Feind auf etwas Ernsthaftes einlassen, wo sie nicht eine reiche Beuthe erwarten können.

*Merz 15*

Auf eine Nachricht, dass eine feindliche Parthey sich sogar erfrechet, dicht an den jenseitigen Ufern des Schuylkill die ausgeschriebene Contribution von denen Einwohnern einzutreiben, wurden die berittenen Jägers unterm Lieut. Mertz beordert, solche zu verfolgen. Diese trafen auch solche an, attaquierten sie, machten 1 Capt., 10 Mann davon gefangen, töteten verschiedene und der Rest rettete sich durch den Wald. Es hatte das feindliche Detachement überhaupt in 80 Mann bestanden.

*Merz 27*

Ein von New York gekommenes Transport Schiff *Brilliant*, mit reconvalescierten und Bagage an Board, hatte das Unglück, in einem starken Sturm Winde nahe bey Philadelphia zu scheitern. Alle Menschen wurden zwar gerettet, die Bagage aber ging verloren.

# ∞ 1778 ∞

*March 12*

A small detachment of Britishers went on a foraging raid down both banks of the Delaware. They brought in a quantity of hay without encountering the slightest thing. Various roving parties were dispatched from Philadelphia, but they consist of raw, newly established Provincials, who only plunder at the army's expense and never engage in anything serious with the enemy unless they can expect rich booty.

*March 15*

Upon receipt of a report that an audacious party of the enemy were collecting the prescribed contribution from the inhabitants close to the far banks of the Schuylkill, the mounted jägers under Lieutenant Mertz were ordered to pursue them. They did indeed meet up with them, attacked them, took one captain and ten men prisoner, and killed several. The rest saved themselves through the woods. In all, the enemy detachment consisted of eighty men.

*March 27*

Having come from New York, a transport ship, the *Brilliant*, with convalescents and baggage on board, had the misfortune to founder near Philadelphia in a strong gale. Everyone was saved, but the baggage was lost.

Jetzt kamen die friedlichen Vorschläge des Parliaments. Jederman glaubte auf das zu verlässigste, dass solche den Frieden nach sich ziehen würden; und so sicher man sich in dieser Meynung bestärkt hatte, so auffallend und verwundernd kamen uns die abschläglichen verächtlichen Antworten des Congress vor, der alles mit Verachtung übersah, das im geringsten von Independence abginge.

## April 1

Da der Feind alle zu Markt kommenden Land Leuthe mehrentheils durch seine Aufmerksamkeit aufhob, selbiger nicht allein alle ihre Waren abnahm, sondern auch noch dazu auf das grausamste mishandelte, so wurde, um dieses zu verhindern, der Obst. Lt. v. Wurmb befehligt, wöchentlich 3 mal mit dem Jäger Corps aus zu marschieren und die kommenden Markt Leuthe dadurch zu protegieren, welches denn auch geschahe und den gewünschten Effect hatte. Und obgleich diese Art Expedition sehr gefährlich (und zwar um deswillen mit der grössten Vorsicht gemacht werden musste, weilen die Gegenden sehr coupiert und mehrentheils waldig waren, besonders aber weilen der Feind immer zum Voraus wissen konnte zu welcher Stundt des Tages wir ausritten und an keine Unterstützung aus denen Linien der weiten Entfernung halber denken durften), so kam es doch nie zu einer Haupt Affaire, auf die wir sonst immer zum Voraus rechneten, sondern es blieb bey kleinen, aber desto öfteren Scharmützeln.

## May 4

Passierten die sämtlichen hessischen Trouppen die Revue vor dem commandierenden General, der sich über das militärische und propre Aussehen derselben sehr zufrieden ausdrückte.

Parliament's peace proposals now arrived.[1]  Everyone trustingly believed that they would bring peace.  So firmly did we hold this opinion that the negative, contemptuous answers of Congress, which contemptuously disregarded everything deviating in the least from independence, seemed so surprising and astonishing to us.[2]

### April 1

Because the enemy, for the most part, were bothering all the country folk coming to market, not only taking away all their goods but also cruelly mistreating them, Lt. Colonel von Wurmb was ordered to prevent this by marching out three times weekly with the Jäger Corps to protect the people coming to market.  This, then, was done and it had the desired effect.  And though this kind of expedition was very dangerous (it therefore had to be carried out with the greatest caution, for the country was very intersected, the major part wooded, and in particular the enemy were always able to know in advance at what time of the day we would ride out and we could count on no support outside the lines due to the great distance), yet we were never involved in a major affair, which as a rule we always reckoned on beforehand, but continued instead to have small but all the more frequent skirmishes.

### May 4

All the Hessian troops passed in review before the GOC, who expressed himself very satisfied with their neat and military appearance.

*May 7*

Gingen einige bewaffnete Brigantinen und Schoner den Delaware hinauf, verbrannten die feindliche Fregatte *Washington* und *Effingham*, nebst einem 24 Canonen Schiff und einigen kleineren Fahrzeugen, so zu Burlington lagen. Einige Häuser und ein Magazin mit allerley Kriegs Bedürfnissen wurden ebenwohl angesteckt, womit sich die Expedition endigte.

*May 8*

Sir Henry Clinton kam heute in Philadelphia an, um das Commando der Armee zu übernehmen, weilen General Howe nach England zurück berufen worden.

*May 13*

Lief eine Fregatte zu Philadelphia ein, wodurch sich die unvermuthete Gerücht verbreitete, dass Frankreich die Independence der Americaner anerkannt und Handlungs Tractate mit ihnen geschlossen habe.

*May 14*

Die Armee wurde beordert, sich so leicht wie möglich zum Felde zu equipieren und alle schwere Bagage abliefern zu können.

*May 19*

Ein feindliches Commando von 6,000 Mann unterm Marquis de la Fayette hatte sich denen Linien von Philadelphia genähert und war bis Whitemarsh und Chestnuts Hill vorgerückt. Ein starkes Corps wurde dahero diesen Abend von der Armee detachiert, um am

*May 7*

Some armed brigantines and schooners went up the Delaware and set fire to the enemy frigates *Washington* and *Effingham,* as well as to a 24-gun ship and some smaller vessels, which lay at Burlington. Some houses and a magazine with various kinds of war materiel were also set on fire, and this completed the expedition.

*May 8*

Today Sir Henry Clinton arrived in Philadelphia to assume command of the army, as General Howe has been recalled to England.

*May 13*

A frigate arrived at Philadelphia, giving rise to the unexpected rumour that France had recognised the independence of the Americans and had concluded trade treaties with them.[3]

*May 14*

The army was ordered to equip itself as lightly as possible for the field and to be ready to deliver up all heavy baggage.

*May 18*

An enemy command of 6,000 men under the Marquis de la Fayette approached the lines of Philadelphia, advancing to Whitemarsh and Chestnut Hill. A strong corps was therefore detached from the army this evening to march up the Schuylkill and to cut off the enemy if possible. On this occasion a detachment of jägers under Captain Ewald formed the van.

Schuylkill hinauf zu marschieren und wo möglich den Feind zu coupieren. Ein Detachement Jägers unterm Capt. Ewald machte hiebey die Avantgarde.

*May 20*

Die Armee rückte diesen Morgen aus und marschierte unterm General Lt. von Knyphausen nach Chesnuts Hill. Der Marquis de la Fayette hatte von unseren Bewegungen Nachricht erhalten und sich durch den Schuylkill eiligst zurück gezogen. Die leichten englischen Dragoner, welche mit dem ersten Corps marschiert waren, fielen noch in die feindliche Arrière und machten verschiedene Gefangene.

Dass die ganze Armee ausrückte geschah, um des Willen weilen der commandierende General en chef willens gewesen, insofern la Fayette abgeschnitten werden können, den General Washington in seynem Lager zu attaquieren, da aber dieses nicht gelang, so marschierte die Armee gegen Abend wieder nach Philadelphia zurück.

*May 24*

Ging Sir William Howe an board des Kriegs Schiffes *Europa*, um nach England zu gehen, und Sir Henry Clinton commandiert nunmehro als General en chef.

*May 25*

Die schwere Bagage der Armee wurde an board derer Schiffe gebracht.

*May 26*

Alle Weibe, Kranke, Marode pp. gingen gleichfalls heute an die Schiffe und die Armee musste parat seyn, zu irgend einer Stunde marschieren zu können.

*May 20*

This morning the army moved out and marched under Lt. Gen. von Knyphausen to Chestnut Hill. The Marquis de la Fayette had received news of our movements and had hastily withdrawn across the Schuylkill. The British Light Dragoons, who had marched with the first corps, nevertheless fell upon the enemy's rear and took several prisoners.

The entire army moved out, for, had it been possible to cut off la Fayette, the GOC in Chief would have been prepared to attack Washington in his camp, but as this did not succeed, the army marched back again to Philadelphia towards evening.

*May 24*

Sir William Howe went on board the ship of war *Europe* to go to England and Sir Henry Clinton now commands as GOC in Chief.

*May 25*

The heavy baggage of the army was taken on board the ships.

*May 26*

Today all women and those who were sick or unfit boarded the ships, and the army had to be ready to march at any hour.

*May 29-31*

The ships sailed from Philadelphia and only a few vessels remained there to await the departure of the army.

*May 29-31*

Segelten die Schiffe von Philadelphia und nur wenige Fahr Zeuge blieben da, um den Abmarsch der Armee zu erwarten.

*Juny 5*

Kamen die englischen Commissars in Philadelphia an, um den Frieden zu schliessen; alle ihre Bemühungen waren aber umsonst, weil die Americaner sich zu sehr auf Frankreich verliessen und keinerley Art von Vorschlägen accepteren wollten.

*Juny 16 und 17*

Verliess die Armee Philadelphia und ging über den Delaware bey Coopers Ferry nach der Jersey über.

*Juny 18*

Heute verliess der Rest der Trouppen die Stadt und wurden selbige bey Gloucester Point übergesetzt. Die feindliche Armee machte nicht die geringste Miene uns in dem Übergehen zu beunruhigen, sondern hielt sich in ihrem Lager ganz stille, war aber parat auf den ersten Wink zu marschieren.

*Juny 17*

General Lieut. von Knyphausen setzte sich mit folgenden Trouppen nach Haddonfield in Marsch: Hessische Jägers *à la tête*, Queens Rangers, Hessische Grenadiers, 2 Bat. Jersey Volontairs, Maryland Loyalists, Volontairs of Ireland, und Caledonia Volunteers. Der Rest der Armee blieb noch am Wasser stehen, um erst die Bagage und den Train der

*June 5*

The British Commissioners arrived in Philadelphia to conclude peace, but all their endeavours were in vain, for the Americans were relying too much on France and would not accept any kind of proposals whatever.

*June 16 and 17*

The army quit Philadelphia and crossed the Delaware to Jersey at Cooper's Ferry.

*June 18*

Today the rest of the troops quit the city and were ferried across to Gloucester Point. The enemy army did not show the slightest sign of troubling us during the crossing and kept completely inactive in their camp, though ready to march at the drop of a hat.

*June 17*

Lt, Gen. von Knyphausen set off with the following troops on the march to Haddonfield: Hessian Jägers *à la tête*, Queen's Rangers, Hessian Grenadiers, 2nd Battalion Jersey Volunteers, Maryland Loyalists, Volunteers of Ireland, and Caledonian Volunteers. The rest of the army was still halted at the water, but only to load the army's baggage and train and get them in order. At Haddonfield the jägers encountered the first enemy picket, who fired but immediately ran off.

*June 18*

Maj. Gen. Leslie[4] was given command of a light corps that was to form the van of the army. It consisted of the following

Armee auf zuladen und in Ordnung zu bringen. Bey Haddonfield trafen die Jägers den ersten feindlichen Posten an, der sein Feuer zwar gab, aber sogleich weg lief.

*Juny 18*

Der General Major Leslie erhielt das Commando über ein leichtes Corps, das die Avantgarde der Armee ausmachen sollte und in folgenden Trouppen bestand: Jägers, Queens Rangers, ein Detachement Jersey Volunteers, 7tes, 23tes u. 63tes Regiment. Die Armee selbst marschierte in 2 Colonnen. Die Jägers haranguierten beständig mit einer feindlichen Observations Parthey, welche sich vor ihnen zurück zog und in jedem Defilee, Wald oder Brücke sich wider setzte, auch all Brücken hinter sich abwarf und sonstige Hindernisse in den Weg räumte. Die Avantgarde campierte wegen denen vielen Waldungen in einem Quaree.

*Juny 19*

Um 4 Uhr Morgens marschierte die Armee in der nämlichen Ordnung wie Gestern. Die Avantgarde lagerte sich zu Irish town an der Balley Bridge, welche die Feinde abgeworfen hatten und die Pioneers wieder aufbauen mussten. Vom feindlichen Observations Corps wurde heute ein Capitaine erschossen und wir verlohren einen Jäger todt und einige blessierte.

*Juny 20*

Der Marsch ging heute bis Mount Holly, wo sich die Armee vereinigte und ins Lager ging. Der feindl. General Major Maxwell mit seiner Brigade hatte in diesem Ort gelegen und sich nach Trentown retiriert. Es war ein fester Posten, der sehr leicht and gut hätte defendiert werden können, sie

troops: Jägers, Queen's Rangers, a detachment of the Jersey Volunteers, and the 7th, 23rd[5] and 63rd Regiments. The army itself marched in two columns. The jägers were constantly skirmishing with an enemy observation party that retreated before them, resisting at every defile, wood or bridge. It also demolished every bridge behind it and left other obstacles in the way. The van camped in a square because of the many patches of woodland.

## June 19

The army marched at four o'clock in the morning in the same order as yesterday. The van camped at Irish Town beside the Balley Bridge, which the enemy had destroyed and which the pioneers had to rebuild. A captain of the enemy observation corps was shot today and we lost one jäger killed and some wounded.

## June 20

Today the march reached Mount Holly, where the army joined up and moved into camp. The enemy Maj. Gen. Maxwell had been posted in this place with his brigade and had retired to Trenton. It was a strong post that could have been very easily and well defended, but so hasty must their retreat have been that they had not even destroyed the bridge here.

## June 21

A halt today. The rest of the army joined us here. The Jäger Corps had to camp in the woods here at the head of the army on the road to Trenton. Lieutenant Cornelius was detached with fifty jägers to set fire to some ships lying in Rancocas Creek.

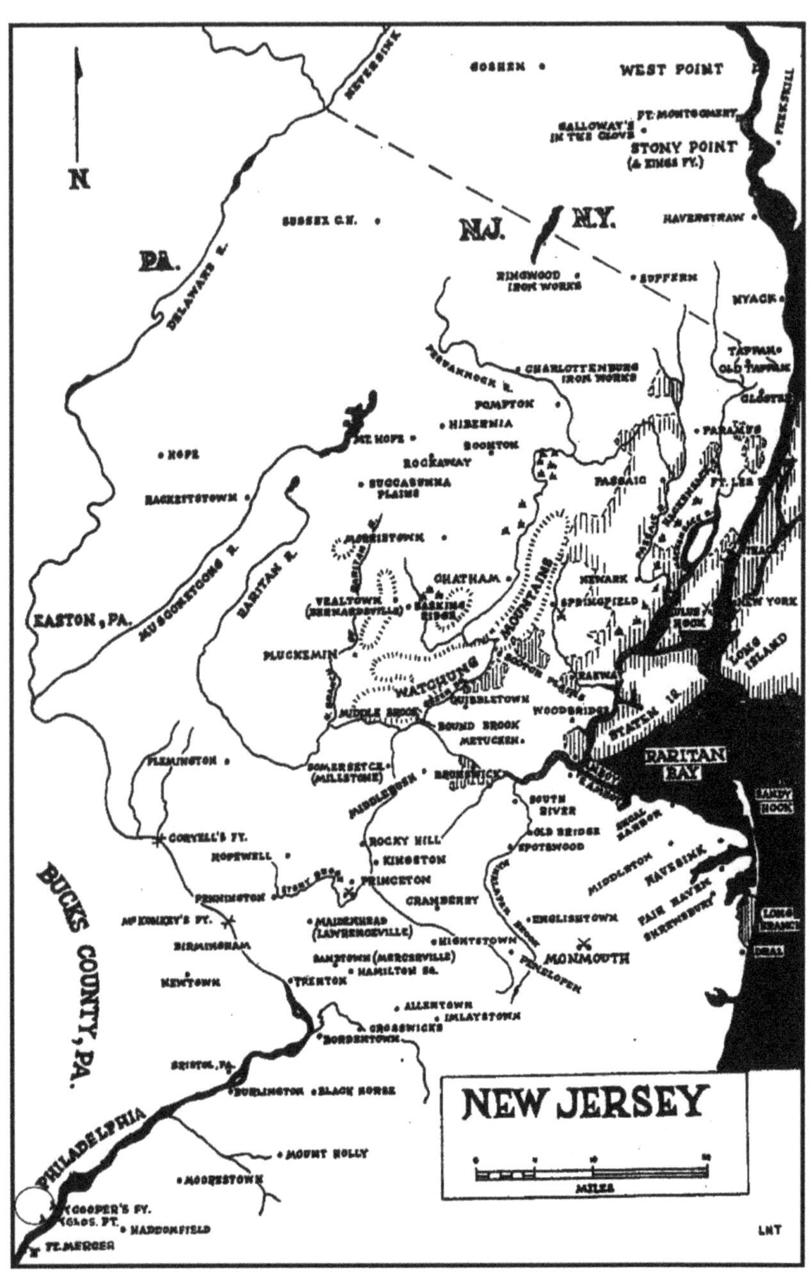

N
NEVERSINK
GOSHEN
WEST POINT
PEEKSKILL
FT. MONTGOMERY
GALLOWAY'S IN THE CLOVE
STONY POINT
(& KING'S FY.)
PA.
SUSSEX C.H.
N.J.
N.Y.
HAVERSTRAW
DELAWARE R.
RINGWOOD IRON WORKS
SUFFERN
NYACK
TAPPAN
OLD TAPPAN
CLOSTER
PEQUANNOCK R.
CHARLOTTENBURG IRON WORKS
POMPTON
HIBERNIA
PARAMUS
MT. HOPE
BOONTON
HOPE
ROCKAWAY
PASSAIC
FT. LEE
HACKETTSTOWN
SUCCASUNNA PLAINS
MUSCONETCONG R.
MORRISTOWN
RARITAN R.
CHATHAM
NEWARK
NEW YORK
EASTON, PA.
VEALTOWN (BERNARDSVILLE)
BASKING RIDGE
SPRINGFIELD
BERGEN POINT
LONG ISLAND
PLUCKEMIN
WATCHUNG MOUNTAINS
QUIBBLETOWN
RAHWAY
MIDDLE BROOK
WOODBRIDGE
STATEN IS.
FLEMINGTON
BOUND BROOK
METUCHEN
SOMERSET C.H. (MILLSTONE)
BRUNSWICK
RARITAN BAY
SANDY HOOK
MIDDLEBUSH
SOUTH RIVER
AMBOY
CORYELL'S FY.
ROCKY HILL
OLD BRIDGE
SPOTSWOOD
MIDDLETOWN
NAVESINK
HOPEWELL
KINGSTON
STONY BROOK
PRINCETON
PENNINGTON
CRANBERRY
FAIR HAVEN
SHREWSBURY
BUCKS COUNTY, PA.
Mc KINLEY'S FY.
MAIDENHEAD (LAWRENCEVILLE)
HIGHTSTOWN
ENGLISHTOWN
LONG BRANCH
BIRMINGHAM
SANDTOWN (MERCERVILLE)
MONMOUTH
PENELOPEN
DEAL
NEWTOWN
HAMILTON SQ.
TRENTON
ALLENTOWN
IMLAYSTOWN
CROSSWICKS
BORDENTOWN
BRISTOL, PA.
PHILADELPHIA
BURLINGTON
BLACK HORSE
NEW JERSEY
MOUNT HOLLY
MOORESTOWN
COOPER'S FY.
GLOS. PT.
HADDONFIELD
FT. MERCER
MILES
LNT

hatten aber hier nicht einmal die Brücke abgebrochen, so eilig musste ihre Retraite gewesen seyn.

*Juny 21*

Rest Tag. Der Rest der Armee stiess hier zu uns und das Jäger Corps musste hier in Front der Armee sich auf der Strasse nach Trentown im Walde lagern und der Lieut. Cornelius wurde mit 50 Jägers detachiert, einige Schiffe, so in Rancocas Creek lagen, zu verbrennen.

*Juny 22*

Heute Morgen 3 Uhr marschierte die Armee in folgender Ordnung: Jägers, Queens Rangers, Pioneers, leichte Infantrie, 2 Wagen Schantz-Zeug, 16 Dragoner, die Grenadiers, 2 12 lb, 1 Haubitze, Garde, 3e Brigade, 3 Bat. von der 4ten Brigade, 6 Pontoons und der Rest des Schantz-Zeugs, die Bagage, die 5e Brigade, Havingdons Provincialen. Ein Bat, der 4ten Brigade flanquierte die Bagage links und Allens Corps rechts. Oberst Dykes Corps marschierte in der Mitte der Bagage und alle übrigen hier nicht benahmten Trouppen marschierten mit der Colonne des Gen. Lt. v. Knyphausen. Zu Springfield machte die Avantgarde halt und deckte die auf der linken Flanque der vorbey defilierenden Armee befindliche Strasse, so nach Trentown führet, damit selbige von dem in Trentown befindl. feindl. Corps von dieser Seite her nicht im Marsch beunruhigt werde, und machte alsdann die Arrière. Das Lager der Armee war zu Black Horse aufgeschlagen. Die Jägers erhielten ihr Emplacement vor dem linken Flügel auf der Trentown Strasse.

*Juny 23*

Die Armee marschierte heute in 2 Colonnen, die eine rechts unter General Lieutenant v. Knyphausen, und die andere

*June 22*

At three o'clock this morning the army marched in the following order: Jägers, Queen's Rangers, Pioneers, light infantry, two waggons with entrenching tools, 16th Dragoons, the Grenadiers, two 12-pounders, one howitzer, the Guards, 3rd Brigade, three battalions of the 4th Brigade, six pontoons and the rest of the entrenching tools, the baggage, the 5th Brigade, and Hovenden's Provincials. A battalion of the 4th Brigade flanked the baggage on the left, and Allen's Corps on the right. Colonel Van Dyke's Corps marched in the centre of the baggage, and all remaining troops not mentioned here marched with Lt. Gen. von Knyphausen's column. At Springfield the van halted. It covered the road to Trenton — which was on the left flank of the army as it filed past — in order to prevent the army on its march from being troubled from that side by the enemy corps in Trenton. It then formed the rear. The camp of the army was pitched at Black Horse. The jägers were assigned their position ahead of the left wing on the Trenton road.

*June 23*

Today the army marched in two columns, the one on the right under Lt. Gen. von Knyphausen and the other on the left under Lord Cornwallis. Leslie's corps formed the van of the column on the left and went to Bordentown, then to the drawbridge over Crosswicks Creek, which had been pulled down. The corps camped there. The jägers were at the head of the corps and occupied the bridge. On the far side of it the enemy had thrown up some flèches, but they were not occupied. Towards evening a detachment of some fifty men threw themselves into these flèches and fired with small arms into the jäger camp. Shortly afterwards Morgan's corps followed this up by cannonading the jägers with two 6-pounders. We remained stationary in our camp, replying

links unter Lord Cornwallis. Das Lesliesche Corps machte die Avantgarde der Colonne links und ging nach Bordentown, hiernächst bis an die Drawbridge (eine Zugbrücke über den Croswick Creek), welche abgeworfen war. Das Corps lagerte sich alda, die Jägers in dessen Front und besetzten die Brücke. Jenseits derselben waren einige flechen vom Feind aufgeworfen, sie waren aber nicht besetzt. Gegen Abend warf sich ein Detachement von ohngefähr 50 Mann in diese Flechen und feuerte mit klein Gewehr in das Jäger Lager und dem folgte bald darauf das Morganische Corps mit 2 6 lb, womit sie die Jägers canonierten. Wir blieben ruhig in unserem Lager liegen und antworteten mit unseren 2 3 lb. Unsere Piquets aber schossen beständig mit Büchsen, bis die einbrechende Nacht dem Feuern ein Ende machte. Wir hatten einige blessierte und unser Pulver Karn war durch eine Canonen Kugel beschädigt.

Spät am Abend zogen wir uns bis hinter die Anhöhe zurück, um uns dem feindl. Canonen Feuer etwa des nächsten Morgens nicht wieder aus zusetzen.

Die rechte Colonne war diesen Morgen zu Croswick auf ein feindliches Corps gestossen, welches eben im Begriffe war die dasige Brücke abzubrechen, wodurch es alda zu einem Scharmützel gekommen, worinnen der Feind sehr gelitten hatte and weg gejagt wurde.

*Juny 24*

Frühe 3 Uhr marschierte das Lesliesche Corps nach Croswick und postierte sich so, dass es der schon im Marsche seyenden Armee die linke Flanque gegen Trentown deckte und nachher die Arrière machte, weilen sich Nachrichten bestätigten, dass die feindliche Armee würklich den

with our two 3-pounders.  However, our pickets were constantly firing with their rifles until nightfall brought the firing to an end.  We had some wounded and our powder cart was damaged by a cannonball.

Late in the evening we withdrew behind rising ground so as not to be exposed again to any enemy cannon fire next morning.

This morning the right-hand column had encountered at Crosswicks an enemy corps that was just about to destroy the bridge there.  This led to a skirmish there in which the enemy suffered severely and were chased off.

## June 24

At three o'clock in the morning Leslie's Corps marched to Crosswicks.  It took post, covering, towards Trenton, the left flank of the army, which was already on the march, and it then formed the rear.  This was because reports were confirmed that the enemy army was indeed crossing the Delaware at Trenton.  In the afternoon parties of other troops were already being sighted at the rear of the Jäger Corps. They had not been observed before and troubled us greatly.  This night the army camped at Englishtown.  The jägers were posted on the high road in front of the centre of the army.

## June 25

Today the march reached Upper Freehold.  Forming the rear, the Jäger Corps was much harassed by the enemy, who pressed particularly hard. We set ambushes for them and these made them very cautious.

Delaware bey Trentown passiere. Am Nachmittag liessen sich auch schon Troops von anderen Trouppen bey der Arrière des Jäger Corps sehen, die man bisher nicht wahr genommen hatte, und die uns sehr beunruhigten. Die Armee lagerte sich diese Nacht bey Englishtown. Die Jägers standen auf der Hauptstrasse vor der Mitte der Armee.

## Juny 25

Der Marsch ging heute bis Upper Freehold. Das Jäger Corps wurde in der Arrière sehr vom Feind belästigt, der besonders heftig aufdrang. Wir legten ihm Embuscaden, die ihn sehr vorsichtig machte.

## Juny 26

Heute marschierte die Armee bis Monmouth, wo sie in einer schönen Ebene das Lager bezog. Die Jägers kamen auf der Strasse von Trentown in einem sehr angenehmen grossen Walde zu stehen. Durch die entsetzliche Hitze verlohren wir 3 Mann. Der Marsch war sehr fatiguant, und da wir als die letzten Trouppen beständig mit dem Feind zu thun hatten und wegen derer erschöpften oder ruinierten Brunnen grossen Mangel an Wasser litten, so fielen viele derer Jäger auf der Strasse um, welche auf denen Pferden derer Officiers, da wir keine Wagen anhalten konnten, mit fortgeschleppt wurden. Dieses trug sich während dieser Retirade über die Jersey sehr öfters zu. Der Feind machte heute zwey sehr lebhafte Attaquen auf unsere Arrière, um sie ab zuschneiden, wurde aber mit Verlust zurück geschlagen. Wir legten ihm eine Embuscade, in welche ein Troop Cavallerie verfiel und wovon verschiedene herunter geschossen wurden.

## Juny 27

Rast Tag. Die feindl. Armee hatte würklich den Delaware passiert und stand bey Cranbury gelagert.

*June 26*

Today the army marched to Monmouth, where it encamped on a beautiful plain. The jägers came to be stationed on the Trenton road in a large, very pleasant wood. We lost three men on account of the dreadful heat. The march was very fatiguing. Being the last troops, we had constantly to deal with the enemy and suffered from a great shortage of water due to the exhausted or spoiled wells. Consequently many of the jägers collapsed on the road and were dragged away on the officers' horses, for we could not procure any waggons. This happened very often during the withdrawal across Jersey. Today the enemy made two very spirited attacks on our rear, which they aimed to cut off, but were driven back with losses. We set an ambush for them. A troop of cavalry fell into it and a number of them were shot down.

*June 27*

A rest day. The enemy army had indeed crossed the Delaware and was encamped at Cranberry.

*June 28*

The army was ordered to march a certain distance in one column. It was then to divide and Lt. Gen. von Knyphausen was to command the column in which the army's baggage and train marched. The jägers were now to form the rear of this column and therefore joined it in Monmouth near the general's quarters at two o'clock in the morning. The 40th Regiment under Lt. Colonel Musgrave and the Jersey Volunteers joined too. The army began to march in this fashion, but the large number of waggons needed a long time before they could all depart. Consequently, when General Washington approached with his army, it was

Die Armee war beordert, in einer Colonne bis auf eine gewisse Distance zu marschieren, wo solche sich dann theilen und der Gen. Lt. v. Knyphausen diejenige commandieren sollte, wo der Train und die Bagage der Armee mit marschierte. Hiervon nun sollten die Jägers die Arrière machen und stiessen deswegen des Nachts um 2 Uhr zu dieser Colonne in Monmouth bey des Generals Quartier, wozu noch das 40e Regmt unterm Oberst Lt. Musgrove und die Jersey Volontaires kamen. Solchergestalt setzte sich die Armee in den Marsch, und da die Menge Wagens eine lange Zeit erforderten ehe solche alle abfahren konnten, war es inzwischen schon gegen 6 Uhr des Morgens als der General Washington mit seiner Armee an marschierte und ihn der General Clinton bloss mit der linken Colonne des Lord Cornwallis erwartete. Der Feind, sobald er auf eine gewisse Distance vor gerücket, rangierte sich in 2 Treffen und General Clinton rückte ihm entgegen und schlug das erste Treffen vollkommen zurück — würde solches auch weiter verfolgt haben, wenn nicht das 2e Treffen, so hinter einem Morast auf einer Anhöhe suf das vortheilhafteste postiert war, ihn daran verhindert hätte. Die englischen Grenadiers machten zwar einen Versuch den Morast zu passieren, liessen aber ihre Canonen darinnen stecken, und brachten solche erst nach vieler Beschwernis wieder heraus. Es wurden in dieser Zeit verschiedene Versuche auf die Bagage gemacht, aber sie misslangen, und da ein starkes Corps gegen unseren Train, der eine grosse Strecke des Weges einnahme, im Anmarsch seyn sollte, so wurden das Jäger Corps und 40es Rgmt. dahin detachiert, um solchen zu decken. Weilen aber der Feind das Corps, in dem er geschlagen, zurück beorderte, so kam es hier zu keiner Affaire. Der General Clinton amüsierte den ganzen Tag über den Feind mit Artillerie Feuer, und da seine Leute zu sehr fatiguiert waren, wollte

already towards six o'clock in the morning and General Clinton awaited him with only Lord Cornwallis's left-hand column. As soon as the enemy had advanced a certain distance, they drew up in two lines and General Clinton marched against them, driving the first line back completely. He would have pursued it farther, had not the second line, which was very advantageously posted behind a morass on rising ground, prevented him from doing so. The British Grenadiers did in fact make an attempt to pass the morass, but their cannon became stuck in it, and they could only get them out after much trouble. Meanwhile various attempts were made upon the baggage, but they failed, and as a strong corps was said to be on the march against our train, which took up a great stretch of the road, the Jäger Corps and 40th Regiment were detached there to cover it. Yet no action ensued here, for the enemy, who had been beaten, recalled the corps. General Clinton amused the enemy with artillery fire the whole day through, and as his men were too fatigued, he was not prepared to attack the enemy a second time in so advantageous a position. He nonetheless had a brigade join him from General Knyphausen's column in case the enemy should attack him, but as this did not occur, he followed with the troops after General von Knyphausen, who had camped not far from Middletown.

In this action the losses on the British side amounted to 320 dead and wounded, and to 600 on the enemy side.

*June 29*

Early this morning Stirn's Brigade was detached to Middletown to occupy the heights there in order to prevent the enemy from doing so. At ten o'clock this evening General Clinton joined up with Lt. Gen. von Knyphausen's column.

er den Feind in einer so vortheilhaften Stellung nicht zum 2en Mal attaquieren, liess aber doch eine Brigade von Gen. Knyphausens Colonne zu sich stossen, im Falle der Feind ihn attaquieren sollte, und da dies nicht geschah, so folgte er mit den Trouppen dem General v. Knyphausen nach, welcher sich ohnfern Middletown gelagert hatte.

Der Verlust englischerseits in dieser Action erstreckte sich auf 320 todt und blessierte und feindl. seits auf 600.

## Juny 29

Die Sternsche Brigade wurde heute früh nach Middletown detachiert, um die dasigen Höhen zu occupieren, damit der Feind solche nicht besezzen könne. Der General Clinton vereinigte sich heute Abend 10 Uhr mit der Colonne des Gen. Lt. von Knyphausen.

## Juny 30

Die Armee marschierte heute mit Tages Anbruch nach Middletown und lagerte sich auf denen Höhen daselbst.

## July 1

Verliess selbige diesen natürlich vesten Posten und nahm eine vortheilhafte Stellung auf denen Höhen zu Navysinck. Die Bagage wurde heute nach der Bay von Sandyhook gebracht, um embarquiert zu werden. Wir erwarteten in dieser Position, so einen halben Mond formierte, einen Angriff des Feindes, es liess sich aber niemand als Morgans Corps von unseren Posten sehen.

General Lee hatte sich mit dem General Washington über die Action des 28en überworfen, indem Lee beschuldigt wurde, dass er ohnnötigerweise retiriert und das erste Treffen nicht in der gehörigen Ordnung angeführt habe.

*June 30*

At daybreak today the army marched to Middletown and camped on the heights there.

*July 1*

The army left this natural strongpoint and took up an advantageous position on the Heights of Navesink. The baggage was taken today to Sandy Hook Bay to be embarked. In this position, which formed a crescent, we awaited an attack by the enemy, but our pickets sighted nothing but Morgan's Corps.

General Lee had fallen out with General Washington over the action of the 28th, Lee being accused of retiring unnecessarily and of not commanding the first line properly.

*July 2, 3 and 4*

The troops remained completely inactive. Meanwhile the baggage was ferried across to Sandy Hook.

*July 5*

No further attack was to be expected from the enemy army here, for it is moving to Brunswick, and from there to the North River to cover the Highlands. The royal army therefore crossed to Sandy Hook today over a pontoon bridge, being taken from there by ship to York, Long and Staten Islands.

The Jäger Corps moved into camp on York Island beside the Eight Mile Stone, but its cavalry had to remain another two days on Sandy Hook (a sandbank on which stands

*July 2, 3, und 4*

Lagen die Trouppen ganz ruhig. Die Bagage wurde inzwischen nach Sandyhook übergesetzt.

*July 5*

Da sich die feindl. Armee nach Braunschweig und von da nach dem Northriver beweget, um die Highlands zu decken, so war von ihr hier kein weiterer Angriff zu erwarten. Die königl. Armee ging daher heute auf einer Schiffs-Brücke nach Sandyhook über, und von da wurde solche zu Schiff nach Newyork, Long und Staatenisland gebracht. Das Jäger Corps kam beym 8 Meilen Stein auf York Island ins Lager, dessen Cavallerie aber musste noch 2 Tage auf Sandyhook (eine Sandbank, worauf nur ein Leucht-Thurm für die Schiffe stehet) blieben und wurde alsdann nach Long Island übergesetzt, woselbst solche abermals verschiedene Tage campierte und nach 8 Tagen wieder zum Corps kam.

*July 9*

Heute ankerte eine französische Flotte von 12 Linien Schiffen und 3 Fregatten zu Sandyhook. Selbige kam vom Delaware, welchen unsere Flotte nur wenige Tage vorher verlassen hatte. Wir erwarteten nichts anderes als einen Angriff auf Newyork, unterdessen sahen wir mit Verlangen dem Admiral Byron entgegen, der denen Franzosen von England gefolgt seyn sollte und eine überlegene Seemacht bey sich habe. Wir machten alle möglichen Anstalten zur Defension.

*July 15*

General Washington hatte den Northriver passiert und sich auf denen Whiteplains gelagert. Das Jäger Corps marschierte vor Kingsbridge und lagerte sich auf dem Spitingdevil. Die

only a lighthouse for the ships). They were then ferried across to Long Island, where they again camped for several days before rejoining the Corps after eight days.

## July 9

Today a French fleet of three frigates and twelve ships of the line anchored at Sandy Hook. It came from the Delaware, which our fleet had left only a few days before. We expected nothing less than an attack on New York, and in the meantime we longed for the arrival of Admiral Byron,[6] who was said to have followed the French from England and to have a superior naval force with him. We made every possible preparation for defence.

## July 15

General Washington had crossed the North River and camped at White Plains. The Jäger Corps marched beyond Kingsbridge and camped on Spuyten Duyvil. The enemy's advanced posts were at Valentine's Hill and Phillipse's House, four miles distant from our outposts.

## July 18

The enemy fleet put to sea again without attempting anything. It is said that Washington is detaching troops to Rhode Island.

The Jäger Corps undertook a patrol to Phillipse's House and encountered there the enemy outpost, which had a very advantageous position on a very steep hill on the other side of the stream. After a few shots had been exchanged, Lt. Colonel von Wurmb withdrew his corps back to camp.

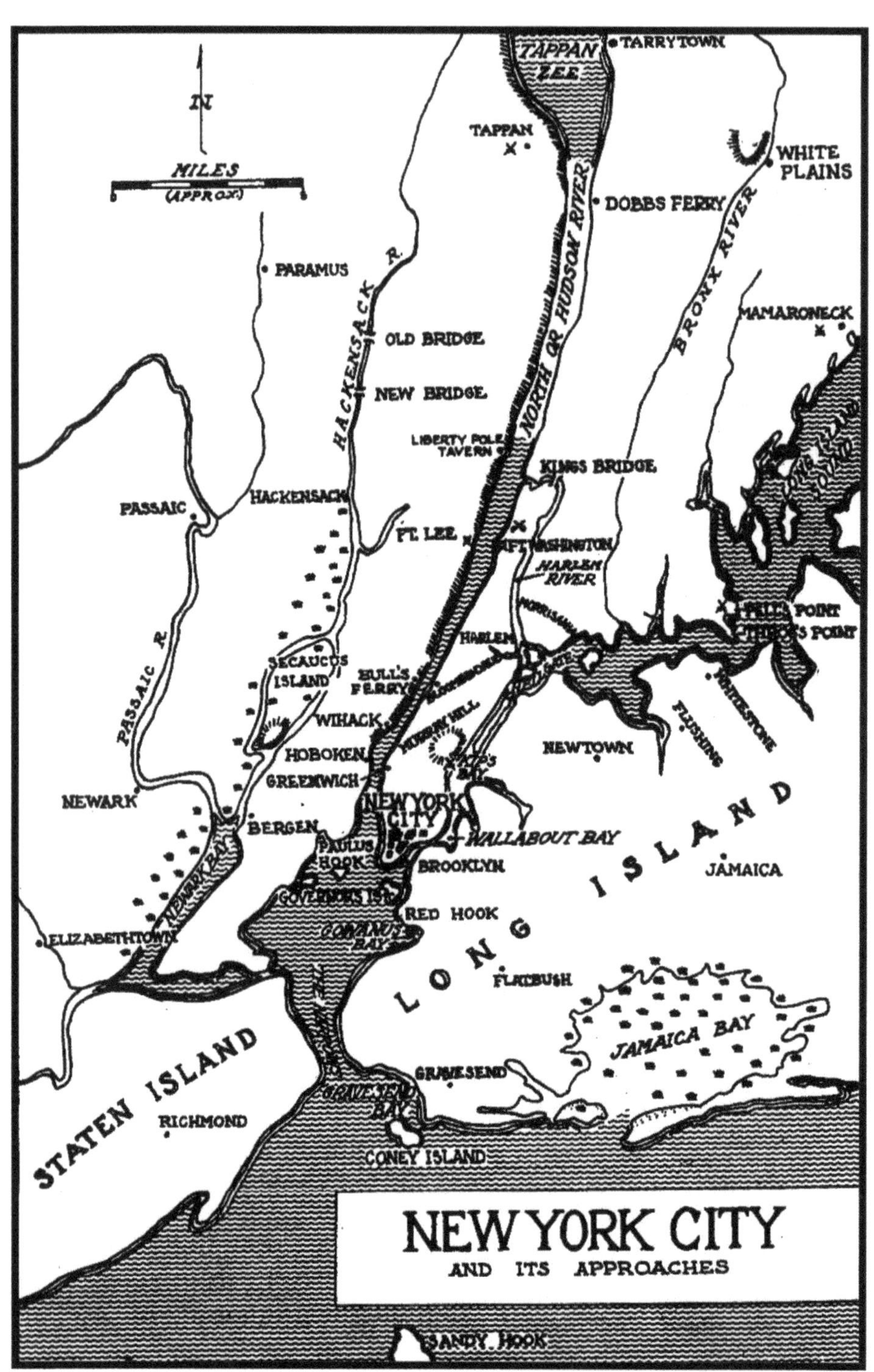


## NEW YORK CITY
### AND ITS APPROACHES

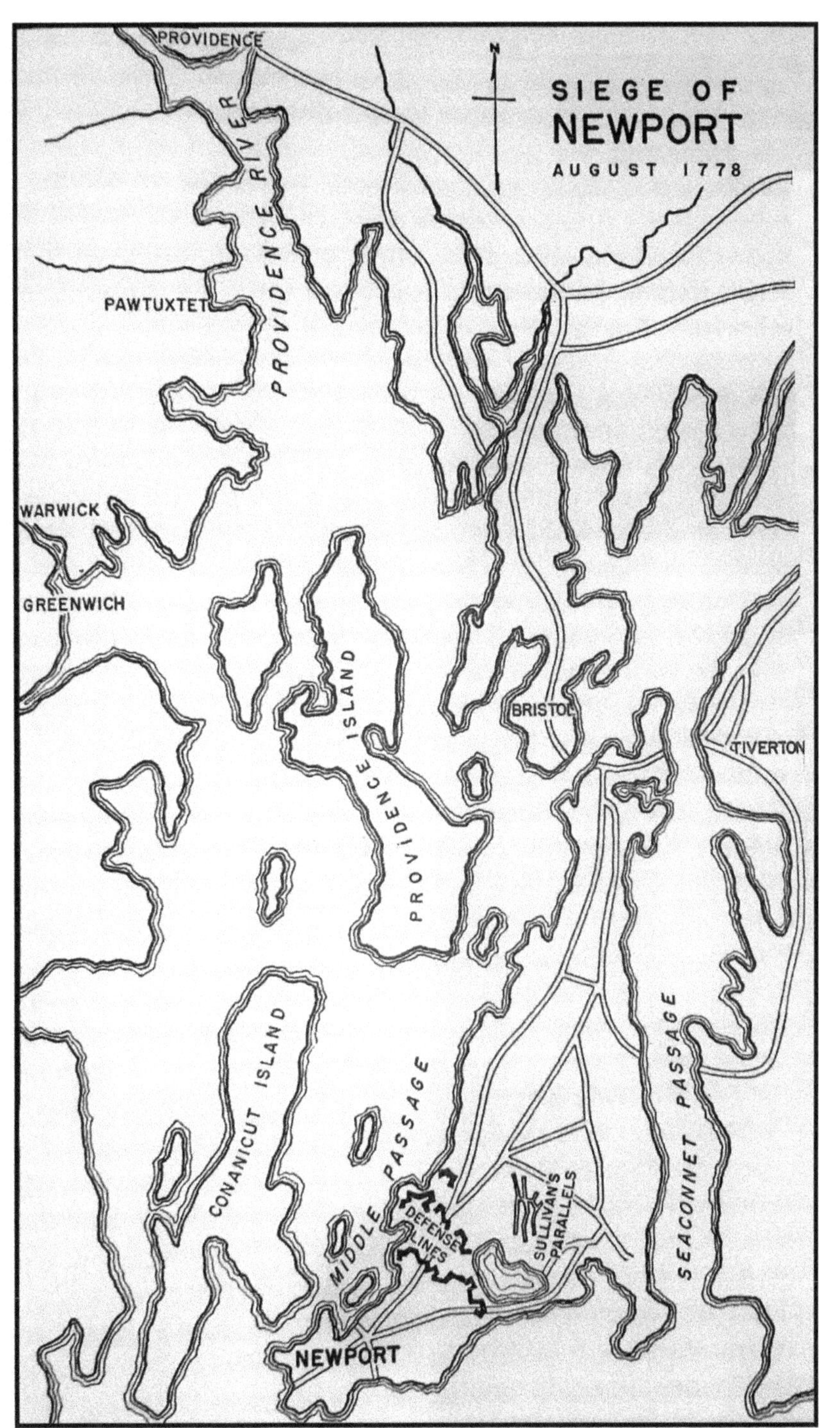


SIEGE OF
NEWPORT
AUGUST 1778
N
PROVIDENCE
PROVIDENCE RIVER
PAWTUXTET
WARWICK
GREENWICH
PROVIDENCE ISLAND
BRISTOL
TIVERTON
CONANICUT ISLAND
MIDDLE PASSAGE
SEACONNET PASSAGE
SULLIVAN'S PARALLELS
DEFENSE LINES
NEWPORT

feindlichen Vorposten standen zu Valentinshill und Philips Haus, 4 Meilen von unseren Posten entfernt.

## July 18

Die feindliche Flotte ging ohne etwas zu unternehmen wieder in See. Man sagt, dass Washington Trouppen nach Rhodeisland detachiere.

Das Jäger Corps machte eine Patrouille bis Philips Haus und traf alda den feindlichen Aussenposten an, der eine sehr vortheilhafte Stellung jenseits des Baches auf einem sehr steilen Berg hatte. Nach einigen wechselseitigen Schüssen zog der Oberst Lt. v. Wurmb sein Corps wieder zurück ins Lager.

## July 26

Die Nachricht, dass Rhodeisland belagert und dass die französische Flotte dahin ab gegangen, scheint sich zu bestätigen. Lord Howe hat inzwischen alle seine Kriegs Schiffe zusammen gezogen, um die Franzosen, so der Comte d'Estaing commandiert, wo nicht zu attaquieren, doch wenigstens so lange zu amüsieren, bis Admiral Byron ankommen werde, welchen wir um deswillen stündlich erwarten dürfen, indem eins seiner Schiffe zu Halifax bereits angekommen.

Vor Rhodeisland ist man sehr besorgt und zweifelt ob die dasige Garnison eine Belagerung werde abhalten können. Die Vestungswerke zu Kingsbridge werden verbessert und neue angelegt, womit sich die Armee jezzo beschäftigt. Die leichten englischen Trouppen campieren in Front derer Redutten auf Hotham's Heights und öftere Scharmützel fallen mit denen feindlichen vor. Das Jäger Corps macht seine Patrouillen auf denen Höhen des Spitingdevils bis vor den feindl. Posten zu Philips Haus. (N.B. Der Spitingdevil ist ein fortdauernder Berg von Kingsbridge, wo ihn die

*July 26*

The report appears to be confirmed that Rhode Island is besieged and that the French fleet has gone there. Meanwhile Lord Howe has gathered all his ships of war, if not to attack the French, who are commanded by Comte d'Estaing, then at least to keep them amused till Admiral Byron arrives, whom we are to expect hourly, for one of his ships has already arrived at Halifax.

People are very concerned about Rhode Island and doubt whether the garrison there will be able to withstand a siege. The fortification works at Kingsbridge are being improved and new ones laid down. The army is busy with this at present. The British light troops are camping in front of the redoubts on Hotham's Heights and frequent skirmishes are taking place with those of the enemy. The Jäger Corps undertakes its patrols on the heights of Spuyten Duyvil up to the enemy post at Phillipse's House. (N.B. Spuyten Duyvil is a continuous hill from Kingbridge, where Harlem Creek cuts it off from York Island, up to Phillipsburg. On its left flows the North River and on the right it is covered for some distance by a branch of Harlem Creek.)

*August 3*

Last night fire broke out in New York, reducing seventy houses to ashes. Many say the fire was started deliberately.

*August 10*

Congress has been obliged to detach a brigade against Colonel Butler,[7] who commands the Indians, and all

Harlems Creek von Yorkisland abschneidet, bis an Philipsburg. Links desselben fliesst der Northriver und rechts wird er von einem Arm des Harlems Creek auf eine gewisse Distance gedeckt.)

### August 3

Verwichene Nacht kam in Newyork Feuer aus, wodurch 70 Häuser in die Asche gelegt wurden. Viele sagen, das Feuer sey angelegt gewesen.

### August 10

Congress ist genötigt gewesen, eine Brigade gegen den Oberst Butler, der die Indianer commandiert, zu detachieren und alle an denen indianischen Grentzen wohnenden Einwohner haben sich flüchtigen müssen, um denen Grausamkeiten derer Wilden zu entgegen.

### August 20

Auf sichere Nachricht, dass die franz. Flotte zwar würklich am 9 Aug. in den Hafen von Rhodeisland eingelaufen, allein am 10 dto., als sich Lord Howe mit seiner Flotte sehen liess, die Anker gelegt und dem Lord entgegen gegangen, auch dass General Sulivan Newport mit 10,000 Mann bloquiert habe — so detachierte der General Clinton 4,000 Mann von der Armee und ging mit selbigen in Person den Sund hinauf, um Rhodeisland zu entsezzen.

### September 7

General Clinton kam heute von Rhodeisland zurück, nachdem solches vom Feind verlassen und die Garnison in Sicherheit war. Er kam mit denen 4,000 Mann unglücklicherweise einen Tag zu spat, um den General Sulivan noch auf der Insul an zutreffen. Dieser, da die franz.

inhabitants on the Indian frontiers have had to flee to escape the cruelties of the savages.

## August 20

There was a reliable report that on 9 August the French fleet had indeed entered the harbour of Rhode Island, but that on the 10th, when Lord Howe and his fleet were sighted, it had weighed anchor and sailed to meet His Lordship — also that General Sullivan[8] had blockaded Newport with 10,000 men. Consequently General Clinton detached 4,000 men from the army and personally proceeded with them up the Sound to relieve Rhode Island.

## September 7

General Clinton arrived back from Rhode Island today after it had been abandoned by the enemy and the garrison was secure. Unfortunately, he arrived with the 4,000 men one day too late to meet up with General Sullivan on the island. The latter raised the siege on 29 August, for the French fleet was no longer prepared to support it, and he was vigorously pursued on his retreat. Lord Howe amused Comte d'Estaing on several occasions with his manœuvres, but as both fleets were scattered by a storm, only single actions took place between several ships. *Le César*, 74 guns, engaged the *Isis*, 50 guns, and had to run for it. The *Renown*, 50 guns, engaged the *Languedoc*, 90 guns, for a long time but in the end had to make off, for six other French ships were approaching. Another action took place between the *Preston* and the *Tonant*, but none was conclusive. Meanwhile the French fleet had reassembled and gone to Boston. Ours remained at Rhode Island till the 4,000 men who had come with General Clinton came back from Martha's Vineyard. They had gone there under Maj. Gen. Grey to fetch cattle for the fleet and army.

Flotte die Belagerung nicht weiter unter stüzzen wollte, hob solche den 29 August auf und wurde in seiner Retirade heftig verfolgt. Lord Howe hatte den Comte d'Estaing durch seine Manœuvres verschiedentlich amüsiert und da beyde Flotten durch einen Sturm zerstreuet geworden, fielen nur einzelne Gefechts zwischen verschiedenen Schiffen vor. Die *Le César* 74 engagierte die *Isis* von 50 Canonen und musste davon laufen. Die *Renown* von 50 engagierte die *Langedoc* von 90 Canonen für eine geraume Zeit, musste aber am Ende sich davon machen, weilen sich 6 andere franz. Schiffe näherten. Ein anderes Gefecht zwischen der *Preston* und der *Tonant* fiel vor, es war aber keins entscheidend. Die franz. Flotte hatte sich inzwischen ressembliert und war nach Boston gegangen. Die unsrige blieb zu Rhodeisland, bis die mit dem General Clinton gegangenen 4,000 Mann wieder von Marthas Winyard zurück kamen, die unterm General Major Grey dahin gegangen, um Vieh vor die Flotte und Armee zu holen. Die Einwohner dieser Insul, so in der Buzzard Bay liegt, verstanden sich hiezu willig, lieferten auch alle ihre Gewehre ab mit dem Vorbehalt, dass sie nicht geplündert würden.

### September 16

Diese Nacht gingen 200 Jägers unterm Major von Prüschenk nach Philipshaus und überrumpelten das dasige Piquet. Die Queens Rangers waren einen anderen Weg marschiert, um den Feind zu coupieren. Beyde Detachements kamen auch zur bestimten Zeit richtig an, der Feind wurde es aber zu früh gewahr und verlohr nur 2 Offr. 28 Mann, so gefangen wurden.

### September 18

Die feindl. Armee ist in Bewegung und ziehet sich nach denen Whiteplains zurück.

The inhabitants of this island, which lies in Buzzards Bay, consented to this willingly and they also delivered up all their arms with the proviso that they would not be plundered.

*September 16*

This night 200 jägers under Major von Prueschenk went to Phillipse's House and surprised the picket there. The Queen's Rangers had marched by another route to cut off the enemy. Both detachments ariived exactly at the appointed time, but the enemy became aware of things too soon and lost only two officers and twenty-eight men, who were captured.

*September 18*

The enemy army is in motion and withdrawing to White Plains.

*September 20*

Maj. Gen. Grey came back from Martha's Vineyard with the 4,000 men.

*September 22*

The enemy army is posted as follows: headquarters at Peekskill, General Gates on the borders of New England, a corps in Newcastle Dstrict, and the advanced posts under General Scott at Tarrytown.

*September 23*

One part of the army marched today under Lt. Gen. von Knyphausen to Phillipse's House, extending the camp from

*September 20*

Kam der Gen. Maj. Grey mit denen 4,000 Mann von Marthas Wineyard zurück.

*September 22*

Die feindl. Armee hat sich folgender massen postiert: Hauptquartier zu Pekskill, General Gates auf den Grenzen von New England, ein Corps in Newcastle District, und die Vorposten unterm Gen. Scott zu Terrytown.

*September 23*

Ein Theil der Armee marschierte heute unterm General Lieut. v. Knyphausen nach Philips Haus und extendierte das Lager vom North bis an den Brunx River auf denen Höhen von Philips und Valentines Haus. Die Jägers standen vor dem linken Flügel am North River. Der andere Theil der Armee unterm General Clinton war in die Jersey gegangen und hatte sich bey der Newbridge gelagert.

*September 28*

Heute Nacht hatte ein Detachement der leichten Infanterie ein Rgmt. feindl. Dragoner in der Jersey überfallen und zu Gefangenen gemacht. Sie hiessen Lady Washingtons Dragoner und waren ohngefähr 100 Mann stark. Die Queens Rangers, welche, die leichte Infanterie zu unterstüzzen, Nachts vorher über den North River gegangen, kamen wieder zurück und bezogen ihr Lager auf dem rechten Flügel, welches während deren Abwesenheit durch 120 Jäger (Capt. Ewald) besezt gewesen war.

*September 30*

Eine Patrouille von 80 Jägers zu Fuss unterm Capt. Donop nebst dem Lieut. Merz mit 12 Cavalleristen gingen heute

the North to the Bronx Rivers on the heights of Phillipse's House and Valentine's House. The jägers were stationed in front of the left wing by the North River. The other part of the army under General Clinton had gone to Jersey, camping at New Bridge.

### September 28

Tonight a detachment of light infantry made a surprise attack on a regiment of enemy dragoons in Jersey and took them prisoner. They were called Lady Washington's Dragoons and were about a hundred strong. The Queen's Rangers, who had crossed the North River the night before to support the light infantry, came back and moved on the right wing into their camp, which had been occupied in their absence by 120 jägers (Capt. Ewald).

### September 30

Early today a patrol of eighty jägers on foot under Captain von Donop went with Lieutenant Mertz and twelve cavalrymen towards Dobbs Ferry to cover the foragers. A detachment under Major Lee lay in ambush and cut off from the main corps both the cavalry and an advanced platoon of the infantry consisting of Lieutenant Bickell and twenty men. Lieutenant Mertz tried to beat his way through with the cavalry but was unable to do so, for he was surrounded by the enemy on foot and on horseback. He surrendered after he himself had been wounded and three of his men hacked to death. By retiring through the woods the infantry lost only five men captured and had two wounded. The enemy was much too strong for Captain von Donop to have been able to do anything. He remained on the other side of the defile with the rest of the patrol, and as Lieutenant Mertz had been captured, he withdrew. The entire corps moved out on hearing the

früh nach Dobbs Ferry, um die Fourageurs zu decken. Ein Detachement unterm Major Lee hatte sich embusquiert und schnitt die Cavallerie nebst einem avancierten Zug der Infanterie, bestehend in Lieut. Bickel und 20 Mann, von dem Haupt Corps ab. Der Lieut. Merz suchte zwar sich mit der Cavallerie durch zu schmeissen, allein er konnte es nicht, weilen er vom Feind zu Fuss und zu Pferdt umringt war, sondern ergab sich, nachdem er selbst blessiert und 3 seiner Leute todt gehauen waren. Die Infanterie verlohr nur 5 Mann gefangen und hatte 2 blessierte, indem sich solche durch den Wald retirierte. Der Feind war zwar zu stark, als das der Capt. von Donop etwas hätte thun können, sondern dieser blieb jenseits des Defilee mit dem Rest der Patrouille stehen und zog sich, da der Lieut. Merz gefangen, zurück. Das ganze Corps rückte zwar auf das Lärmen aus, kam aber zu spat, weil sich der Feind sogleich retiriert hatte.

*October 1*

Das Jäger Corps, Queens Rangers, Legion und Emerichs Corps (sämtliche unterm Comando des Oberst Lt. v. Wurmb) marschierten diese Nacht, erstere die Sawmill River Strasse und die Engländer über Tuckeyhoe, um ein feindl. Corps, so bey Hammonds Haus stand, zu über fallen, unglücklicher weise aber fiel das Jäger Corps des Morgens gegen 4 Uhr auf ein Piquet, von dem man nichts wusste. Dieses gab Feuer und avertierte dadurch den Feind von unserer Ankunft, welcher sich auch sogleich zurück zog und dadurch entging. Die Trouppen retournierten noch den selbigen Abend und waren von dem langen Marsch sehr ermüdet.

*October 3*

Heute früh 10 Uhr alarmierte eine feindl. Patrouille die Vorposten derer Grenadiers am Sawmill River und nach

din but arrived too late, for the enemy had immediately retired.

## *October 1*

The Jäger Corps, Queen's Rangers, Legion[9] and Emmerich's Corps (all under the command of Lt. Colonel von Wurmb) marched this night, the former by the Sawmill River road and the British via Tuckahoe, to make a surprise attack on an enemy corps lying at Hammond's House, but unfortunately, towards four o'clock in the morning, the Jäger Corps fell in with a picket of which we knew nothing. The picket fired, warning the enemy of our arrival, who at once withdrew and thus escaped. The troops returned the same evening and were very tired from the long march.

## *October 3*

At ten o'clock this morning an enemy patrol turned out the advanced posts of the Grenadiers at Sawmill River, and after a few shots had been exchanged, it hastily withdrew.

## *October 4*

According to reports, the main enemy corps is at Quaker Hill, two brigades are at Northbury,[10] and General Scott is with a flying corps and cavalry at Bedford. From this position it may be easily deduced that Washington is not disposed to attack New York, as had been rumoured.

## *October 10*

Today the army marched back to Kingsbridge and into its former camp. The light troops returned to Spuyten Duyvil and Hotham's Heights.

einigen gewechselten Schüssen zog sich selbige eiligst wieder zurück.

*October 4*

Nachrichten zufolge stehet das feindl. Haupt Corps zu Quakerhill, 2 Brigaden zu Northberry, und General Scott mit einem fliegenden Corps und Cavallerie zu Bedford. Aus dieser Stellung lässt sich leicht schliessen, dass Washington nicht intentioniert sey, Newyork, so wie man aus gesprengt hatte, zu attaquieren.

*October 10*

Die Armee marschierte heute in ihr voriges Lager nach Kingsbridge zurück und die leichten Trouppen gingen wieder auf Spitingdevil und Hothams Heights.

*October 13*

Eine feindliche Cavallerie Patrouille allarmierte heute das Jäger Corps und machte uns einen Posten gefangen, zog sich aber sogleich wieder zurück.

*October 14*

Die englische Flotte präpariert sich, nach denen West Indies zu gehen, womit 4,000 Engländer unterm Gen. Maj. Grand embarquiert wurden.

*November 6*

Eine andere Expedition von ohngefähr 2,500 Mann, nem. 1 Bat. vom 71 Rgmt., Delancys Corps, York Volontairs, und die Rgmtr. v. Wissenbach und Welwarth, wurden heute embarquiert, deren Bestimmung geheim blieb.

*October 13*

Today an enemy cavalry patrol turned out the Jäger Corps, capturing one of our pickets, but retired immediately.[11]

*October 14*

The British fleet is preparing to sail to the West Indies and 4,000 Britishers have been embarked under Maj. Gen. Grant.

*November 6*

Another expedition of some 2,500 men, namely one battalion of the 71st Regiment, De Lancey's Corps, York Volunteers, and the Regiments von Wissenbach and Woellwarth, embarked today. Their destination remains secret.

*November 13*

Today we received a report that the enemy's army had moved into winter quarters and that the headquarters were at Chatham in Jersey.

*November 16*

The royal army moved into winter quarters on York, Long and Staten Islands. The jägers came to Flushing on Long Island — the officers were given houses, but the men had to build huts for themselves, being supplied with nails and tools.

*November 29*

Upon receipt of information that the prisoners of Burgoyne's army were to be transported from New

*November 13*

Heute erhielten wir Nachricht, dass die feindl. Armee ihre Winter Quartiere bezogen und dass das Haupt Quartier zu Chatham in der Jersey sey.

*November 16*

Die königl. Armee bezog die Winter Quartiere auf York-, Long- und Staatenisland. Die Jägers kamen nach Flushing auf Long Island — die Offiziers erhielten Häuser, die Leuthe aber mussten sich Hütten bauen, wozu ihnen Nägel und Arbeitszeug geliefert wurden.

*November 29*

Auf erhaltene Nachricht, dass die Gefangenen der Burgoyne Armee von New England nach Virginien transportiert werden sollten und am Kingsferry den North River passieren müssen, marschierten die British Grenadiers, leichte Infanterie und Rgmt. v. Mirbach nach Tarrytown, kamen aber zu spat, weilen die Trouppen schon würklich den North River 10 Stunden vorher passiert hatten. Die Ursache warum diese Trouppen nach Virginien geschickt worden ist, weilen ihnen die Newengländer keine Provision mehr geben wollen.

So endigte sich die Campagne des Jahres 1778: beyde Armeen waren ruhig in ihren Winterquartieren, nichts wurde beyderseitig unternommen, und wir richten unser Augenmerk und zugleich unsere Hoffnungen auf die Operationen in denen West Indies.

England to Virginia and would have to cross the North River at Kings Ferry, the British Grenadiers, light infantry and the Regiment von Mirbach marched to Tarrytown but they arrived too late, for the troops had in fact crossed the North River ten hours earlier. The reason for these troops being sent to Virginia is that the New Englanders are no longer willing to give them provisions.

And so ended the campaign of 1778: both armies were inactive in their winter quarters, nothing was undertaken on either side, and we directed our attention, and at the same time our hopes, to the operations in the West Indies.

# ∞ 1779 ∞

*January 1*

Da die Provision der Armee alle erschöpft und die schon lange erwartete Cork Flotte noch nicht eingelaufen, so fing es an, daran zu mangeln. Es wurde dahero auch die Hälfte Hafermehl statt des Brods geliefert und vom 8ten bis 20ten January emfing die Armee Zwieback von Hafer Mehl gebaken.

*January 18*

Kame die Provisions Flotte von Cork an.

*February 7*

Heute erhielten wir die angenehme Nachricht, dass die königliche Flotte unterm Rear Admiral Barrington in denen West Indies St. Lucia denen Franzosen weg genommen habe:

> Die engl. Flotte verliess Barbadoes am 12ten Dec. 1778 und ankerte im Grand cul de Sac den 13ten frühe, landete die Trouppen die Nacht und nahmen Possession von der Insul den 14ten frühe ohne Widerstand. Den nemlichen Nachmittag kam die franz. Flotte unter Mr. D'Estaing und machte den 15ten eine Attaque auf die englische, so in der Bay lag, hielte sich aber zu sehr entfernt, um grossen Schaden zu thun, und legte sich gegen Abend auf eine gewisse Distance vor Anker. Den 16ten waren die Franzosen beständig unter Segel und landeten ihre Trouppen. Den 18ten machten solche eine Attaque auf die Engländer am Lande, wurden

## ∞ 1779 ∞

### January 1

There began to be a shortage of provisions, for the army's stocks were all exhausted and the long awaited fleet from Cork had not yet arrived. Consequently half rations of oatmeal were supplied instead of bread and from 8 to 20 January the army received Zwieback[1] baked from oatmeal.

### January 18

The provision fleet arrived from Cork.

### February 7

Today we received the welcome news that the royal fleet under Rear Admiral Barrington[2] had taken St. Lucia in the West Indies from the French:

> The British fleet left Barbadoes on 12 December 1778 and anchored in the Grand Cul de Sac early on the 13th. It landed the troops during the night and took possession of the island early on the 14th without opposition. The same afternoon the French fleet under Monsieur d'Estaing arrived. On the 15th it made an attack on the British fleet lying in the bay, but kept too far off to do any great harm, and towards evening cast anchor some distance away. On the 16th the French were constantly under sail and landed their troops. On the 18th they attacked the British on land but were repulsed by Maj. Gen. Medows,[3] notwithstanding that they twice stormed the British lines.

aber durch den General Major Meadows zurück geschlagen,
ohngeachtet sie zu 2 Malen die englischen Linien stürmten.
Den 24ten verliess d'Estaing, nachdem die Land Trouppen
reembarquiert und nichts ausgerichtet hatten, die Insul und
segelte nach Port Royal.

## *February 13*

Vom Oberst Campel erhielten wir gleichfalls die gute
Nachricht, dass er mit denen am 6 Novbr. von York
gesegelten Trouppen Besitz von Georgien genommen und
die dasigen feindl. Trouppen unterm General Howe bey
Savannah geschlagen habe:

Oberst Campbel kam den 23 Dez. nach vielem bösen Wetter
bey der Insul Tybee an, ging den Savannah Fluss bis nach
Gerardots Plantage hinauf, welches der erste practicable
Landungsplatz war. Hier debarquierte er die Trouppen den
27. 50 Rebellen waren daselbst postiert und gaben ihr Feuer,
wurden aber weg gejagt und der Landungsplatz gesichert.
General Maj. Howe, der die Americaner comandierte, war
am östlichen Ende der Stadt Savannah auf marschiert, wo
ihn sofort der Oberst Campel attaquierte und in die Flucht
schlug. Er war ohngefähr 4,000 Mann stark und machte nun
so geschwinde Retirade durch den Wald, dass nur wenige
Gefangene gemacht wurden.

## *May 1*

Das 42nd Rgmt., Prinz Carl und Lord Rawdons Corps und
die Grenadier Compagnie der Garde wurden unterm Brig.
Gen. Mathew embarquiert, um an der Küste von Virginien
und hauptsächlich in der Chesapeak Bay die feindlichen
Magazine und Schiffe zu ruinieren.

After re-embarking the land troops, who had accomplished nothing, d'Estaing left the island on the 24th and sailed to Port Royal.

## February 13

We also received from Colonel Campbell[4] the good news that he had taken possession of Georgia with the troops who had sailed from New York on 6 November, and had defeated at Savannah the enemy troops there under General Howe:[5]

> After much bad weather Colonel Campbell arrived off the island of Tybee on 23 December and went up the Savannah River to Girardeau's plantation, which was the first practicable landing place. Here he disembarked the troops on the 27th. Fifty rebels were posted there and opened fire, but they were chased away and the landing place secured. Maj. Gen. Howe, who commanded the Americans, was drawn up at the eastern end of the town of Savannah, where he was instantly attacked by Colonel Campbell and put to flight. He had about 4,000 men and made such a rapid retreat through the forest that only a few prisoners were taken.

## May 1

The 42nd Regiment, Prinz Carl, Lord Rawdon's Corps, and the grenadier company of the Guards were embarked under Brig. Gen. Mathew[6] to destroy the enemy's magazines and ships on the coast of Virginia and mainly in Chesapeake Bay,

Wurde die Armee beordert, sich heute jenseits Kingsbridge zu ressemblieren und alda ein Lager zu beziehen. Die in Cantonierung liegenden Rgmtr. und Corps brachen dahero mit Tages Anbruch auf, passierten die Kingsbridge um 7 Uhr des Morgens und marschierten in folgender Ordnung:

Nach Philipshaus: reitende Jägers (N.B. diese waren von Flushing aus über Brooklyn marschiert und hatten allda den Eastriver passiert), die hessischen Grenadiers und Rgmt. v. Bose;

Nach Williamsbridge: Queens Rangers, Legion, 7 u. 63 Rgmt;

Nach Valentines Hill: Fergusons Corps, leichte Infanterie, 17 Dragoner und Robinsons Corps;

Nach Miles square: Emerichs Corps, 17, 23, 33 u. 64 Rgmt.

Die Fuss Jägers marschierten von Flushing nach Whitestone, passierten daselbst den East River und marschierten über Westchester nach Philips House. Die englischen Grenadiers marschierten gleichfalls von Jamaica den nämlichen Weg nach Whitestone, passierten nach dem Jäger Corps den Fluss und gingen darauf nach Eastchester ins Lager.

*May 29*

The army was ordered to reassemble today beyond Kingbridge and to move into camp there. Consequently the regiments and corps lying in cantonments set off at daybreak. They passed Kingsbridge at seven o'clock in the morning and marched in the following order:

> To Phillipse's House: mounted jägers (N.B. these had marched from Flushing via Brooklyn and had crossed the East River there), the Hessian Grenadiers, and the Regiment von Bose;
>
> To Williamsbridge: Queen's Rangers, Legion, 7th and 63rd Regiments;
>
> To Valentine's Hill: Ferguson's Corps, light infantry, 17th Dragoons, and Robinson's Corps;
>
> To Mile Square: Emmerich's Corps, 17th, 23rd, 33rd, and 64th Regiments.

The foot jägers marched from Flushing to Whitestone, crossed the East River there, and marched via Westchester to Phillipse's House. The British Grenadiers also marched the same route from Jamaica to Whitestone, crossed the river after the Jäger Corps, and then went into camp at Eastchester.

The army camped in the following order:

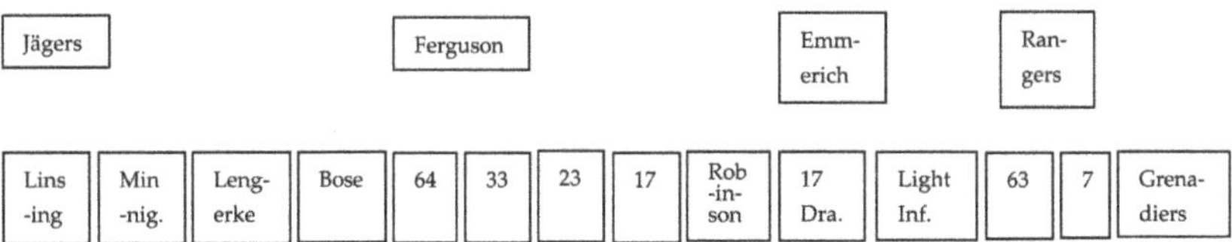

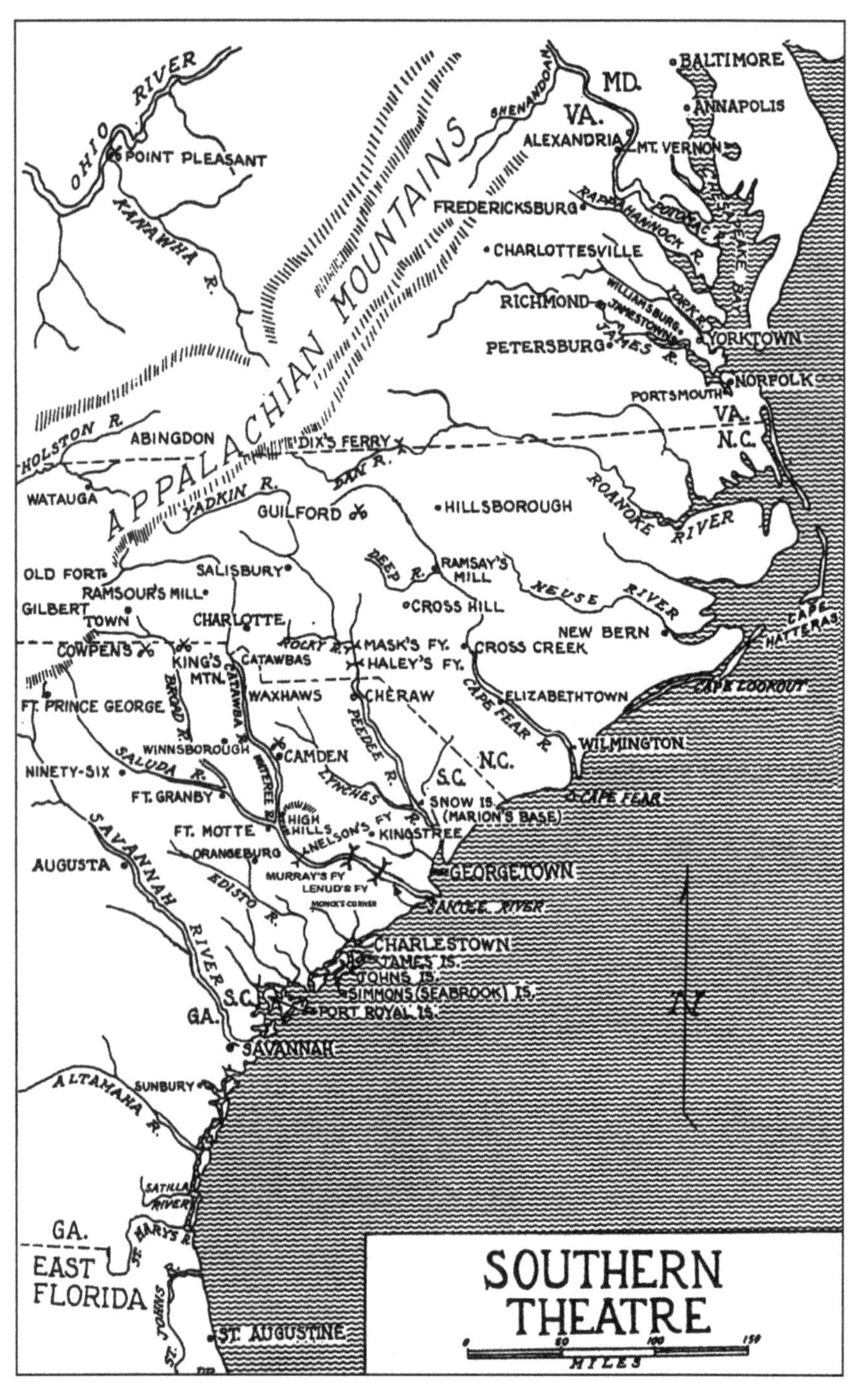

OHIO RIVER
POINT PLEASANT
KANAWHA R.
HOLSTON R.
SHENANDOAH
BLUE RIDGE
APPALACHIAN MOUNTAINS
MD.
VA.
BALTIMORE
ANNAPOLIS
ALEXANDRIA
MT. VERNON
FREDERICKSBURG
RAPPAHANNOCK R.
POTOMAC R.
CHESAPEAKE
CHARLOTTESVILLE
RICHMOND
WILLIAMSBURG
JAMESTOWN
YORK R.
YORKTOWN
PETERSBURG
JAMES R.
NORFOLK
PORTSMOUTH
VA.
N.C.
ABINGDON
DIX'S FERRY
DAN R.
HILLSBOROUGH
ROANOKE RIVER
WATAUGA
YADKIN R.
GUILFORD
OLD FORT
SALISBURY
DEEP R.
RAMSAY'S MILL
NEUSE RIVER
RAMSOUR'S MILL
GILBERT TOWN
CHARLOTTE
CROSS HILL
NEW BERN
CAPE HATTERAS
COWPENS
KING'S MTN.
CATAWBAS
ROCKY R.
MASK'S FY.
HALEY'S FY.
CROSS CREEK
CAPE LOOKOUT
FT. PRINCE GEORGE
BROAD R.
CATAWBA R.
WAXHAWS
CHERAW
ELIZABETHTOWN
PEEDEE R.
CAPE FEAR R.
WILMINGTON
WINNSBOROUGH
CAMDEN
N.C.
SALUDA R.
WATEREE R.
LYNCHES R.
S.C.
NINETY-SIX
FT. GRANBY
SNOW IS.
(MARION'S BASE)
CAPE FEAR
FT. MOTTE
HIGH HILLS
NELSON'S
KINGSTREE
SAVANNAH RIVER
ORANGEBURG
EDISTO R.
MURRAY'S FY
LENUD'S FY
GEORGETOWN
AUGUSTA
MONCK'S CORNER
SANTEE RIVER
CHARLESTOWN
JAMES IS.
JOHNS IS.
SIMMONS (SEABROOK) IS.
S.C.
PORT ROYAL IS.
GA.
SAVANNAH
ALTAMAHA R.
SUNBURY
N
GA.
EAST FLORIDA
SATILLA RIVER
ST. MARYS R.
ST. JOHNS R.
ST. AUGUSTINE
SOUTHERN THEATRE
0        50        100        150
MILES

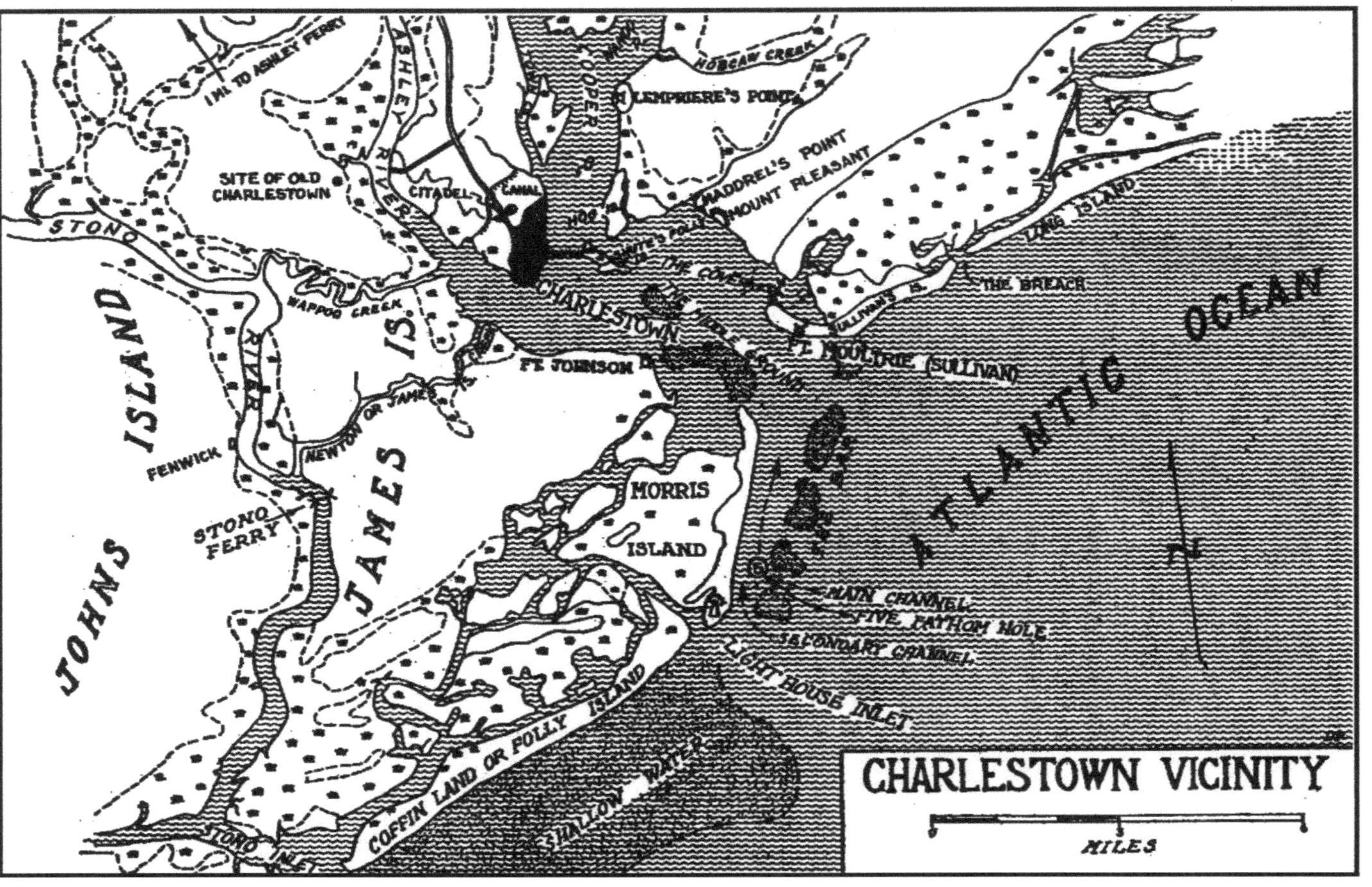

CHARLESTOWN VICINITY
MILES
ATLANTIC OCEAN
JOHNS ISLAND
JAMES IS.
STONO
SITE OF OLD CHARLESTOWN
1 MI. TO ASHLEY FERRY
ASHLEY RIVER
CITADEL
CANAL
COOPER R.
HOGAN CREEK
LEMPRIERE'S POINT
HADDREL'S POINT
MOUNT PLEASANT
LONG ISLAND
THE BREACH
SULLIVAN IS.
FT. MOULTRIE (SULLIVAN)
CHARLESTOWN
WAPPOO CREEK
FT. JOHNSON
FENWICK
NEWTON OR JAMES CREEK
STONO FERRY
MORRIS ISLAND
MAIN CHANNEL
FIVE FATHOM HOLE
SECONDARY CHANNEL
LIGHT-HOUSE INLET
SHALLOW WATER
COFFIN LAND OR FOLLY ISLAND
STONO INLET
N

Die Armee campierte folgendergestalt:

| Jägers | | | | | | Ferguson | | | | | Emm-erich | | Ran-gers |
| --- | --- | --- | --- | --- | --- | --- | --- | --- | --- | --- | --- | --- | --- |

| Lins-ing | Min-ig. | Leng-erke | Bose | 64 | 33 | 23 | 17 | Rob-in-son | 17 Dra. | Light Inf. | 63 | 7 | Grena-diers |
| --- | --- | --- | --- | --- | --- | --- | --- | --- | --- | --- | --- | --- | --- |

Der rechte Flügel erstreckte sich vom East River zum Brunx River, das Centrum vom Brunx zum Sawmill, und der linke Flügel von da bis zum Northriver. General Major Vaughan commandierte die engl. Trouppen, General Major von Kosboth die Hessen, und General Major Erskine die sämtlichen leichten Trouppen der Armee.

## May 30

Diesen Nachmittag 1 Uhr kam der B. Genl. Mathew mit seinem Detachement aus Virginien zurück und legte sich bey Philips House vor Anker. Er hatte vor 6 Tagen Portsmouth verlassen, viele Schiffe genommen und verbrandt, und eine ansehnliche Beute gemacht.

Folgende Trouppen wurden beordert, sogleich bey Philips House embarquieren zu können: engl. u. hessische Grenadiers, Legion zu Fuss, Robinsons Corps, leichte Infanterie, 17, 63 u. 64tes Rgmt., nebst 300 Jägers unterm Major von Prüschenk. Das Embarquement war gegen 10 Uhr geendigt.

## May 31

Um 2 Uhr diesen Morgen segelten die ein geschifften Trouppen den North River hinauf und ankerten um 11 Uhr zu Fertrite Hook (auch Tallers Point genannt). Gleich darauf debarquierten 100 Jägers, das 17, 63 u. 64te Rgmt., nebst

The right wing extended from the East to the Bronx River, the centre from the Bronx to the Sawmill, and the left wing from there to the North River. Maj. Gen. Vaughan commanded the British troops, Maj. Gen. von Kospoth the Hessians, and Maj. Gen. Erskine[7] all the army's light troops.

### May 30

At one o'clock this afternoon Brig. Gen. Mathew arrived back with his detachment from Virginia and cast anchor off Phillipse's House. He had left Portsmouth six days ago and had taken and burnt many ships,. He had also acquired considerable booty.

The following troops were ordered to be ready at once to embark off Phillipse's House: British and Hessian Grenadiers, Legion infantry, Robinson's Corps, light infantry, 17th, 63rd and 64th Regiments, together with 300 jägers under Major von Prueschenk. The embarkation was completed towards ten o'clock.

### May 31

At two o'clock this morning the troops who had embarked sailed up the North River and at eleven o'clock anchored at Verdrietige Hook (also called Tallers Point).[8] Immediately afterwards one hundred jägers, the 17th, 63rd, and 64th Regiments, together with Robinson's Corps, disembarked on the west bank at Stoney Point, where a party of the enemy at once abandoned some works which had been started but not yet completed. Maj. Gen. Paterson,[9] who commanded this detachment, took possession of them, throwing up a battery immediately, whilst Maj. Gen. Vaughan landed the rest of the troops on the eastern bank at Verplanck's Point, where the enemy had built Fort La

Robinsons Corps, auf dem westlichen Ufer zu Stoney Point, alwo im Detachmt. der Feind einige angefangene aber noch nicht fertige Werke sogleich verliess. Der General Major Paterson, der dieses Detachment commandierte, nahm davon Besitz und warf sogleich eine Batterie auf, während dem der General Major Vaughan den Rest derer Trouppen auf dem östl. Ufer zu Verplankspoint landete, wo der Feind das Forth la Fayette erbaut und mit einem Detachement besetzt hatte. Dieses wurde durch den Gen. Vaughan bloquiert.

General Major Erskine, der den Rest der Armee bey Philipshouse commandierte, brach mit demselben gegen 10 Uhr Vormittags auf und rückte bis auf die Höhe von Dobbs Ferry vor, wo er dergestalt Posto fasste, dass der rechte Flügel durch die Höhen von Sawmill und der linke vom Northriver gedeckt wurde.

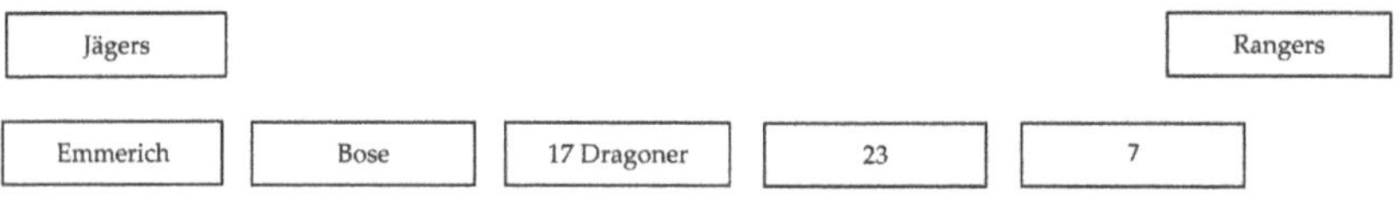


## Juny 1

General Major Patterson eröffnete diesen Morgen mit Tages Anbruch eine Batterie von 1 12 lb und einer Haubitze von Stoneypoint gegen das Forth la Fayette, mit so gutem Effect, dass sich der darin commandierende feindl. Capitaine mit 4 Subalterns und 70 Mann gegen 10 Uhr ergab. Das Forth war ein regulaires $4^t$ mit doppelten Verpallisadierungen und Gräben versehen.

General Erskine machte heute mit der Cavallerie eine Patrouille bis jenseits denen Whiteplains, um den Feind zu recognoscieren und allenfalls die Bewegungen des Gen. Gates, der in Providence stand, zu observieren, allein er

Fayette and occupied it with a detachment. This was blockaded by General Vaughan.

Maj. Gen. Erskine, who commanded the rest of the army at Phillipse' House, set off with it towards ten o'clock in the morning, advancing till he was level with Dobbs Ferry, where he took post with the right wing covered by the heights of Sawmill and the left by those of the North River.

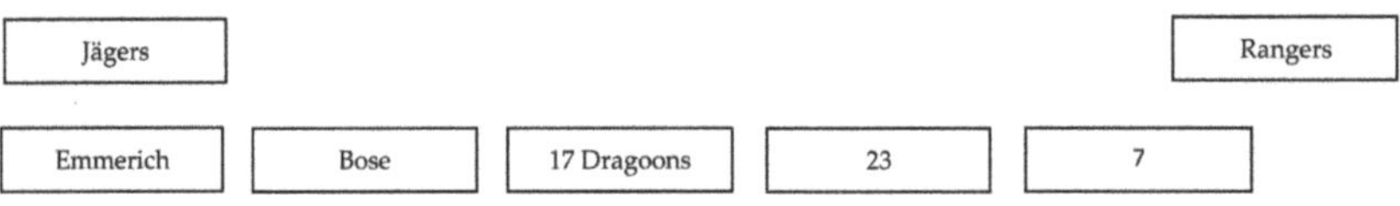


## June 1

At daybreak this morning Maj. Gen. Paterson opened fire upon Fort La Fayette from Stoney Point with a battery of one 12-pounder and one howitzer. The effect was so good that the enemy captain commanding there surrendered towards ten o'clock with four subalterns and seventy men. The fort was a regular square provided with double palisades and ditches.

Today General Erskine undertook a patrol with the cavalry beyond White Plains to reconnoitre the enemy and possibly observe the movements of General Gates[10], who was stationed in Providence. He was, however, unable to obtain any reliable information or to discover anything of the enemy.

## June 3

After news had come in that the enemy had collected a number of cattle on the Croton River to supply their army and to deny them to ours, General Erskine, leaving behind

konnte weder sichere Nachricht erhalten, noch vom Feinde selbst etwas entdecken.

*Juny 3*

Auf eingelaufene Nachricht, dass der Feind eine Anzahl Vieh am Crodon River zusammen getrieben habe, um seine Armee damit zu versehen und uns solches zu entziehen, marschierte General Erskine mit der Cavallerie, Jägers, Rangers, 23ten Rgmt. und 200 Mann vom Rgmt. von Bose, mit Zurücklassung aller Bagage, um 11 Uhr nach Singsing, wo das 23e Rgmt. und Bosesches Detachement auf der Strasse nach Whiteplains postiert wurden. Die übrigen Trouppen marschierten auf der Northcastle Strasse fort. Die Cavallerie und Rangers nahmen das Vieh, nebst der dabey befindlichen Wache von 18 Mann, weg und trieben solches zurück nach dem Lager zu Dobbs Ferry, um es zum Behufe der königlichen Hospitäler zu employieren. Das Jäger Corps machte beym Zurück Marche, so in der Nacht geschah, die Arrière und wurde nicht verfolgt.

*Juny 4*

Die Armee celebrierte heute des Königs Geburtstag, indem solche ausrückte und ein Freuden Feuer machte.

*Juny 5*

Das 42te Rgmt., Prinz Carl und Lord Rawdons Corps kamen heute von Stoneypoint zurück und rückten in das alte Lager der Armee bey Philips Haus. Das Corps des Gen. Maj. Erskine marschierte ebenwohl von Dobbs Ferry dahin.

*Juny 6*

General Clinton kam heute vom Stoneypoint und recognoscierte die Linie bey Philips Hause und nahm darauf sein Quartier in Philipsburgh.

all the baggage, marched at eleven o'clock with the cavalry, jägers, Rangers, 23rd Regiment and 200 men of the Regiment von Bose to Sing Sing, where the 23rd Regiment and Bose detachment were posted on the road to White Plains.  The other troops marched ahead on the North Castle road. The cavalry and Rangers seized the cattle and the guard of eighteen men who were there and drove the former back to the camp at Dobbs Ferry for the use of the royal hospitals.  On the return march, which took place during the night, the Jäger Corps formed the rear and was not pursued.

*June 4*

Today the army celebrated The King's birthday by marching out and firing a *feu de joie*.

*June 5*

Today the 42nd Regiment, Prinz Carl, and Lord Rawdon's Corps came back from Stoney Point and moved into the army's old camp at Phillipse's House.  Maj. Gen. Erskine's corps also marched there from Dobbs Ferry.

*June 6*

Today General Clinton came from Stoney Point and reconnoitred the line at Phillipse's House.  Afterwards he took up his quarters in Phillipsburg.

*June 7*

According to reports the enemy army has at last moved from Jersey towards West Point to defend Fort Defiance and the Highlands.

*Juny 7*

Die feindliche Armee hat sich endlich, Nachrichten zufolge, aus der Jersey gegen Westpoint bewegt, um das Forth Defyance und die Highlands zu vertheidigen.

*Juny 8*

General Major Erskine machte heute eine Patrouille mit der Cavallerie nach denen Whiteplains, traf einige Miliz zu North Castle an, machte 9 davon Gefangen, einige wurden nieder gehauen, und abermals eine Anzahl Vieh weg genommen. Des feindl. Obersten Thomas Haus mit allen darin befindlichen Meublen wurde bey dieser Gelegenheit verbrannt, weilen er als ein Gefangener seine ihm gegebene Parole gebrochen und ein Rgmt. Miliz commandierte ohne ausgewechselt zu seyn.

*Juny 11*

Da die neu angelegten Werke zu Stoneypoint beynahe fertig sind, so wurden heute schwere Canonen auf dem Northriver dahin gebracht.

*Juny 15*

Das Jäger Corps und Rangers machten heute Patrouillen, der Feind kam aber nie weiter herunter bis an die Crodon Brücke, bis wohin er seine Patrouillen schickte.

*Juny 17*

Eine gestern Abend von Georgien angekommene Sloop brachte die Nachricht mit, dass der General Major Prevost von Savannah aus bis in die Nachbarschaft von Charlestown vorgerückt sey, dass er am 8en May Besitz von Sullivans

*June 8*

Today Maj. Gen. Erskine undertook a patrol with the cavalry to White Plains and fell in with some militia at North Castle. He took nine of them prisoner, some were cut down, and once again a number of cattle were seized. On this occasion the house of the enemy Colonel Thomas[11] was burnt with all the furniture in it, for he had broken the parole granted to him as a prisoner and was commanding a regiment of militia without being exchanged.

*June 11*

As the works recently begun at Stoney Point are almost completed, heavy cannon were taken there today along the North River.

*June 15*

The Jäger Corps and Rangers undertook patrols today, but the enemy never came down farther than the Croton Bridge, to which they sent their patrols.

*June 17*

A sloop arriving yesterday evenng from Georgia brought news that Maj. Gen. Prevost[12] had advanced from Savannah to the vicinity of Charlestown, had taken possession of Sullivan's Island and Fort Johnson on 8 May, and was now making preparations to besiege Charlestown.

*June 18*

General Washington is in camp in Smith's Clove and is said to have a very weak army with him. General Gates is still

Island und Forth Johnston genommen und nunmehro Anstalten mache, Charlestown zu belagern.

*Juny 18*

General Washington stehet in denen Smiths Cloves im Lager and soll eine sehr schwache Armee bey sich haben. Der General Gates mit denen New Engländern stehet noch immer in Providence, um die Grenzen von New England zu decken.

*Juny 19*

Im Platz des General Major Erskine, so nach England zurück gehet, commandiert nunmehro der General Maj. Mathew die zu Philipsburgh gelagerten Trouppen.

*Juny 24*

Der Oberstlieutenant von Wurmb erhielt den Auftrag, mit denen leichten Trouppen die feindlichen Aussenposten zu recognoscieren und womöglich solche zu überfallen, und Nachrichten von der Armee einzuziehen. Die Queens Rangers mussten dahero nach Pontsbridge verwichene Nacht marschieren. und die Legion ging selbigen zur rechten, um einem zu Crambond stehenden feindlichen Corps den Pass nach Bedford abzuschneiden; der Feind hatte sich aber schon Tags vorher zurück gezogen und einige Meilen weiter fort einen kleinen Posten von 40 Mann gelassen, der durch die Rangers gefangen wurde. Das Jäger Corps marschierte nach Horton's Heights und das 17e Dragoner Rgmt. rechts demselben über die White Plains. David's Hill (derjenige Ort, wo die feindl. Armee in 1776, als der General Howe attaquierte, im Lager stand) war das bestimmte Rendezvous. Hier vereinigten sich die

in Providence with the New Englanders to cover the borders of New England.

*June 19*

Maj. Gen Mathew now commands the troops encamped at Phillipsburg in place of Maj. Gen. Erskine, who is going back to England.

*June 24*

Lt. Colonel von Wurmb received orders to reconnoitre the enemy outposts with the light troops, to make a surprise attack on them if possible, and to gather information about the army.  The Queen's Rangers had therefore to march to Pine's Bridge last night and the Legion went to their right to cut off the pass to Bedford that lay open to an enemy corps stationed at Crompond; but the enemy had already retired the day before, leaving a small outpost of forty men a few miles farther on, which was captured by the Rangers. The Jäger Corps marched to Horton's Heights and the 17th Dragoons marched to their right beyond White Plains. David's Hill (the same place where the enemy army was in camp in 1776 when General Howe attacked) was the appointed rendezvous.  The jägers and 17th Dragoons joined up here towards one o'clock midday, having encountered nothing of the enemy on their lines of march. At four o'clock in the afternoon an enemy cavalry patrol was spotted and pursued by our cavalry, but they could not overtake it.  Next morning the Rangers and Legion joined up with the rest of the troops on David's Hill, and as all enemy outposts retired, Lt. Colonel von Wurmb remained here simply to gather further intelligence and to re-await the scouts who had been sent out.  Then he marched

Jägers und 17e Dragoner des Mittags gegen 1 Uhr, ohne dass beyde an ihrer Marschroute etwas feindliches angetroffen hatten. Des Nachmittags 4 Uhr liess sich eine feindl. Cavallerie Patrouille sehen. Dieser wurde zwar mit unserer Cavallerie nachgesetzt, konnte sie aber nicht einholen. Des nächsten Morgens vereinigten sich die Rangers und Legion mit denen übrigen Trouppen auf David's Hill, und da sich alle feindlichen Vorposten zurück zogen, so blieb der Oberst Lt. von Wurmb hier stehen, um erst noch einige Nachrichten ein zu ziehen und die ausgeschickten Kundschafter erst wieder abzuwarten — und marschierte alsdann

*Juny 26*

in das Lager nach Philips Haus zurück.

*Juny 27*

Die Werke zu Stoneypoint und Verplanckspoint sind nunmehro fertig und werden auf folgende Weise besetzt:

Stoney Point:  der Oberst Lt. Johnston, 40 Canonen, 100 Artilleristen, 17, 33 Rgmt. und Fergusons Corps

Verplanckspoint:  der Oberst Lt. Webster, 20 Canonen, 40 Artilleristen, 63 Rgmt., Robinson's Corps und 2 Comp. Grenadiers.

Diese Werke decken die Kingsferry, die Haupt Strasse von Boston und ganz New England nach Philadelphia und denen südlichen Provinzen, welches dem Feind grossen Abbruch thut.

Der Rest derer Trouppen embarquierte heute, um sich mit der Armee bey Philipshaus zu vereinigen.

*June 26*

back to the camp at Phillipse's House.

*June 27*

The works at Stoney Point and Verplanck's Point are now ready, being occupied as follows:

> Stoney Point:  Lt. Colonel Johnson,[13] 40 guns, 100 gunners, 17th and 33rd Regiments, and Ferguson's Corps

> Verplanck's Point: Lt. Colonel Webster,[14] 20 guns, 40 gunners, 63rd Regiment, Robinson's Corps, and two companies of Grenadiers.

These works cover Kings Ferry, the main route from Boston and the whole of New England to Philadelphia and the southern provinces, which does the enemy great harm.

The rest of the troops embarked today to join up with the army at Phillipse's House.

*June 28*

The troops who had come from Stoney Point disembarked and moved into their camp in the line.

*June 29*

Last night Lt. Colonel Emmerich[15] surprised a small picket at Byram's Bridge, eleven of whom were killed and the rest captured.

*Juny 28*

Die Trouppen, so von Stoney Point gekommen, debarquierten und bezogen ihr Lager in der Linie der Armee.

*Juny 29*

Der Oberst Lt. Emerich surprisierte verwichene Nacht ein kleines Piquet an der Byrams Bridge, wovon 11 Mann blieben under der Rest gefangen wurde.

*July 1*

Eine Parthey von Staatenisland marschierte verwichene Nacht nach Woodbridge in der Jersey, attaquierte einen kleinen dasigen feindl. Posten, und machte 1 Offr. 12 Dragoner davon gefangen.

*July 2*

Die Cavallerie des Jäger Corps under der Legion und Rangers marschierten heute aus dem Lager bey Philipshaus (unterm Col. Tarleton), um ein feindl. Cavallerie Detachment zu Pondsreach zu überfallen. Den 3en July früh 3 Uhr trafen sie auch den feindl. Posten an. Durch die Unwissenheit des Wegweisers aber, wurde die gerade in das Lager führende Strasse verfehlt, wodurch der Feind Zeit gewann, sich, wiewohl mit zurück lassung vieler Pferdt Sattel und Zeug, zu retirieren. Eine Estandarte, 1 Offr. u. 22 Mann fielen in unsere Hände. Im zurück Marsch wurde die Cavallerie durch die Miliz beunruhigt, thaten aber wenig Schaden.

*July 3*

Verwichene Nacht ging das 7 u. 23 Rgmt. nebst 40 Jäger (unter Lt. Bickel) nach  Frogsneck, um allda zum 54en

## July 1

Last night a party from Staten Island marched to Woodbridge in Jersey and attacked a small enemy post there, taking prisoner one officer and twelve dragoons.

## July 2

The cavalry of the Jäger Corps, and that of the Legion and Rangers, marched out of the camp at Phillipse's House today (under Colonel Tarleton) to surprise an enemy cavalry detachment at Pound Ridge. On 3 July, at three o'clock in the morning, they came upon the enemy post, but through the ignorance of the guide they missed the road leading straight into the camp, thereby giving the enemy time to retire, though many horses, saddles and accoutrements were left behind. One standard, one officer and twenty-two men fell into our hands. On the return march the cavalry were harassed by the militia but they did little harm.

## July 3

Last night the 7th and 23rd Regiments went with forty jägers (under Lieutenant Bickell) to Throgs Neck to join up there with the 54th, the Landgraf Regiment and Fanning's Corps, which had come from Rhode Island yesterday. They were then to go on an expedition under Maj. Gen. Tryon to the coast of New England.

## July 4

The troops under General Tryon proceeded under sail up the sound.

Rgmt., Landgraf und Fannings Corps zu stossen, welche gestern von Rhodeisland gekommen, und alsdann eine Expedition unterm General Major Tryon an der Coast von New England zu machen.

## July 4

Die Trouppen unterm Gen. Tryon gingen unter Segel den Sund hinauf.

## July 5

Die englischen und hessischen Grenadiers, leichte Infanterie, 17 Dragoner, Legion und Rangers erhalten Ordre marschfertig zu seyn.

## July 7

Diesen Morgen früh sezten sich die vorbemeldten Trouppen unterm General Vaughan in Bewegung, marschierten nach Mamaroneck und lagerten sich daselbst, um die zwischen Kingsbridge und diesem Ort employierten Heumacher zu decken.

## July 8

Nachrichten zufolge ist der feindl. General Sullivan mit denen unter ihm stehenden Brigadiers Clinton, Maxwell, Poor, Hand u. Potter am 23 Juny zu Wyoming am Susquehanna an gekommen, um die indianischen Partisans Butler und Brand zu vertreiben.

Aus Savannah hören wir, dass General Prevost mit seiner Armee am 11 May des abends vor Charlestown erschienen, welches den Feind veranlasste die Vorstadt zu verbrennen. Den 12 forderte er die Stadt auf und gab ihr 4 Stunden

## July 5

The British and Hessian Grenadiers, light infantry, 17th Dragoons, Legion and Rangers received orders to be in readiness to march.

## July 7

The afore-mentioned troops were put in motion early this morning under the command of General Vaughan. They marched to Mamaroneck and camped there to cover the haymakers employed between that place and Kingsbridge.

## July 8

According to reports the enemy General Sullivan, together with Brigadiers Clinton, Maxwell, Poor, Hand and Potter, who are under his command, arrived on 23 June at Wyoming on the Susquehanna to expel the Indian partisans Butler and Brant.

We hear from Savannah that on the evening of 11 May General Prevost appeared with his army before Charlestown, which caused the enemy to burn the outskirts. On the 12th he summoned the town and gave it four hours to consider. The Town Councillors entered into negotiations to delay the general, knowing that General Lincoln was on the march to protect the town, and this saved them, for, with the approach of the enemy, General Prevost was not prepared to storm the town and had to withdraw to James Island.

## July 14

Maj. Gen. Tryon, who had sailed on 4 July from Throgs Neck with the detachment under his command, issued a

Bedenkzeit. Die Magistratspersonen liessen sich auch auf eine Verhandlung ein, um den General auf zu halten, weilen sie wussten, dass der General Lincoln auf dem Marsch sey, um die Stadt zu schüzzen, und dieses rettete sie, indem General Prevost bey der Annäherung des Feindes die Stadt nicht stürmen wollte, sondern sich nach James Island zurück ziehen musste.

## July 14

General Major Tryon, welcher mit dem unter ihm stehenden Detachement den 4 July von Frogneck segelte, liess seine Proclamation an die Einwohner von New England ergehen, sich den königl. Waffen zu unter werfen, und versprach ihnen alle Protection, wenn sie nur in ihren Häusern ruhig bleiben wollten. Er landete darauf den 5 zu Newhaven, um die Gesinnung der Einwohner zu versuchen, fand aber die Stadt verlassen und eine Verschanzung, Black Rock genannt, welche die Miliz besetzt hatten. Diese wollte er nicht attaquieren, sondern schlug einen Theil des Feindes aus der Stadt heraus, der sich darinnen postiert hatte, verbrannte alle publique Häuser und Magazins, und ging den nächsten Morgen an die Schiffe zurück. Er segelte von da den 6 nach Fairfield, verbrannte die Stadt, da sich die Einwohner alle armiert hatten, re-embarquierte und lief nach Handington Bay. Von da segelte er am 11ten nach Norwalk, legte auch diesen Ort in die Asche, und kam darauf den 12ten nach Whitestone zurück. Die 40 Jägers, so die mehreste Zeit mit der Miliz engagiert waren, hatten 2 todt, 4 blessiert und 3 gefangen.

## July 16

Verwichene Nacht gegen 2 Uhr hörten wir eine kurze Canonade zu Stoneypoint, welches vermuthen liess, dass

proclamation to the inhabitants of New England to submit to the royal forces and promised them every protection if only they would remain peacefully in their homes. Then on the 5th he landed at New Haven to test the temper of the inhabitants, but he found the town deserted and an entrenchment called Black Rock which the militia had occupied. He preferred not to attack it but expelled from the town a part of the enemy who had taken post there, burnt all public buildings and storehouses, and returned to the ships the next morning. On the 6th he sailed from there to Fairfield, burnt the town (for the inhabitants had all armed themselves), re-embarked and moved to Huntington Bay. On the 11th he sailed from there to Norwalk, laid this place too in ashes, and then returned to Whitestone on the 12th. The forty jägers, who for most of the time had been engaged with the militia, had two dead, four wounded, and three taken prisoner.

*July 16*

Towards two o'clock last night we heard a brief cannonade at Stoney Point, from which it was assumed that one of the posts there was being attacked. We were not mistaken and next morning we were astonished to hear that the enemy had attacked and carried Stoney Point.

*July 17*

Maj. Gen. Stirling's brigade was embarked on the North River very early this morning to retake Stoney Point, but they were unable to sail because of the contrary wind. General Vaughan, who had been posted at Mamaroneck to cover the haymakers, retired today to the camp at Phillipse's House, as did Maj. Gen. Tryon with his detachment. Then the Rangers, Legion and 17th Dragoons

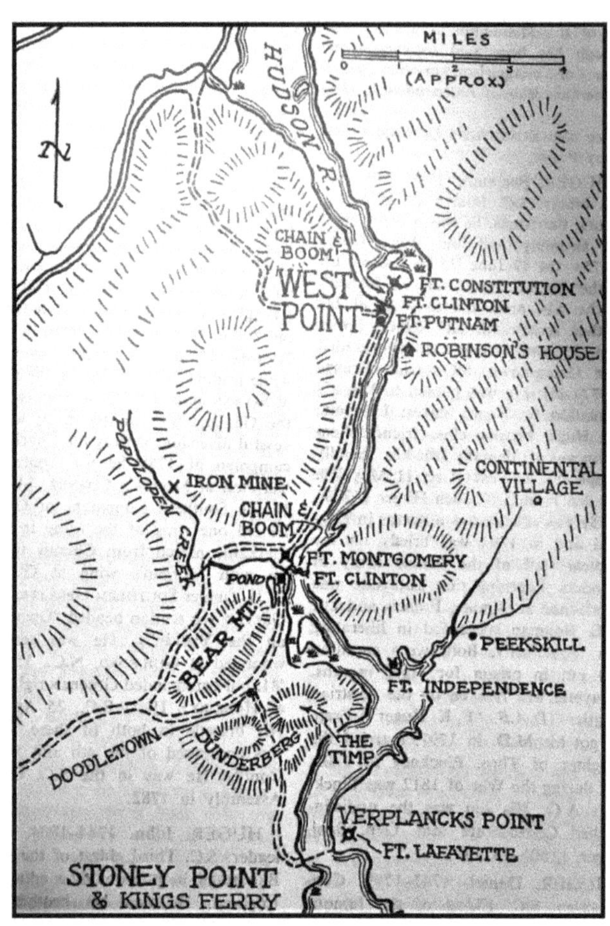

MILES
(APPROX)
HUDSON R.
CHAIN & BOOM
WEST POINT
FT. CONSTITUTION
FT. CLINTON
FT. PUTNAM
ROBINSON'S HOUSE
POPOLOPEN CREEK
IRON MINE
CHAIN & BOOM
CONTINENTAL VILLAGE
POND
FT. MONTGOMERY
FT. CLINTON
BEAR MT.
PEEKSKILL
FT. INDEPENDENCE
DOODLETOWN
DUNDERBERG
THE TIMP
VERPLANCKS POINT
FT. LAFAYETTE
STONEY POINT
& KINGS FERRY


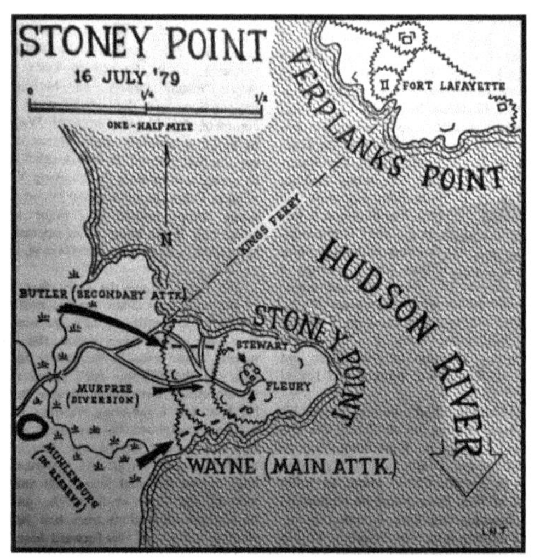

STONEY POINT
16 JULY '79
ONE-HALF MILE
VERPLANKS POINT
FORT LAFAYETTE
KINGS FERRY
HUDSON RIVER
STONEY POINT
BUTLER (SECONDARY ATTK)
STEWART
FLEURY
MURFREE (DIVERSION)
MUHLENBERG (IN RESERVE)
WAYNE (MAIN ATTK)

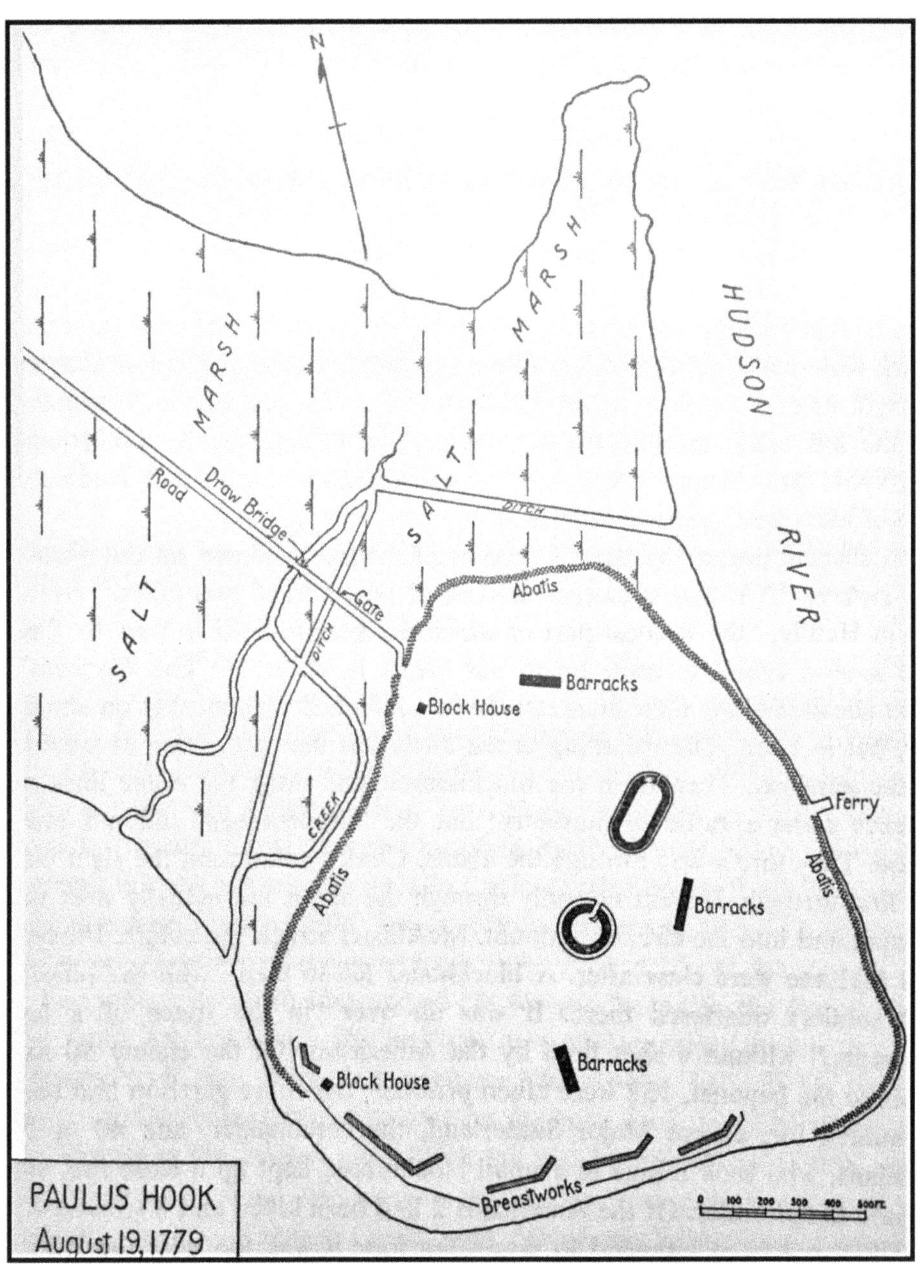
N
MARSH
SALT
MARSH
SALT
HUDSON
RIVER
Road
Draw Bridge
DITCH
Gate
DITCH
CREEK
Abatis
Abatis
Abatis
Barracks
Block House
Ferry
Barracks
Barracks
Block House
Breastworks
0  100  200  300  400  500 FT.
PAULUS HOOK
August 19, 1779

einer derer dasigen Posten attaquiert wurde. Wir betrogen uns darinnen auch nicht und hörten mit Verwunderung des nächsten Morgens, dass der Feind Stoneypoint attaquiert und genommen habe.

### July 17

Die Brigade des General Major Stirling wurde diesen Morgen ganz frühe auf dem Northriver embarquiert, um Stoneypoint wieder weg zunehmen, konnte aber wegen dem widrigen Wind nicht segeln. General Vaughan, der zu Mamaroneck zur Deckung der Heumacher postiert war, zog sich heute ins Lager bey Philipshaus zurück — General Major Tryon mit seinem Detachement desgleichen. Sodann marschierten die Rangers, Legion und 17 Dragoner nach Crombond, um Verplanckspoint, worinnen der Oberst Webster commandierte, zu unterstüzzen, indem solches einem feindl. Angriff durch den Verlust von Stoneypoint sehr ausgesezzt wurde.

### July 18

Die Armee marschierte nach Dobbs Ferry und nahm eben die Stellung, so ein Theil derselben vorher am 31 May bey der ersten Wegnahme von Stoneypoint genommen hatte, um die Operationen gegen diesen Ort auch jezzo wieder zu unterstüzzen. Einige Fregatten waren inzwischen bereits den Fluss hinaufgegangen, und ehe noch einmal der General Major Stirling ankam, hatte der Feind den Posten schon wieder abandoniert, er hatte aber alle Artillerie, bis auf einige schwere Stücke, mit genommen. Jedoch wurde ihm eine Schaluppe mit 11 Canonen an Bord wieder abgenommen, weilen selbige bey eintretender Ebbe auf den Sand gesegelt.

### July 19

Die Brigade Stirling re-occupierte Stoneypoint und die Werke, die der Feind wegen der Kürze der Zeit nicht völlig

marched to Crompond to support Verplanck's Point, where Colonel Webster commanded, for, by the loss of Stoney Point, it was much exposed to an enemy attack.

## July 18

To support once more the operations against Stoney Point, the army marched to Dobbs Ferry and occupied exactly the position that part of it had previously occupied on 31 May when Stoney Point was first carried. In the meantime some frigates had already gone up the river, and even before Maj. Gen. Stirling[16] arrived, the enemy had again abandoned the post, though they had taken all the artillery with them except a few heavy pieces. However, a sloop with eleven cannon on board was retaken, for it had sailed on to the sand as the ebb-tide set in.

## July 19

Stirling's brigade reoccupied Stoney Point, and the works, which the enemy had not completely destroyed due to shortage of time, were repaired. The enemy General Wayne[17] made the following report to General Washington about this affair:

> At midday on 15 July he marched from Sandy Beach (thirteen miles distant) with 1,200 picked troops, arriving at eight o'clock in the evening at Mr Springsteel's farm, one and a half miles from the fort. Here they formed up and halted until they had reconnoitred the works. At half past eleven he ordered the troops to advance. On the right wing 150 volunteers formed the van under Colonel Fleury,[18] who was preceded by one officer and twenty men with axes to clear away the palisades. And on the left wing this detachment consisted of 100 volunteers under Major Stewart[19] with one officer and twenty pioneers. These advanced detachments

ruinert, wurden ausgebessert. Der feindl. General Wayne machte folgenden Rapport an den General Washington über diese Affaire:

Er marschierte mit 1,200 ausgesuchten Trouppen von Sandybeach (13 Meilen entfernt) am 15 July des Mittags 12 Uhr und kam des Abends 8 Uhr auf Mr Springfields Plantage, 1½ Meilen vom Forth, an. Hier formierte er sich und machte Halt bis er die Werke recognosciert hatte. Um ½ 12 Uhr liess er die Trouppen avancieren. Auf dem rechten Flügel machten 150 Freiwillige unterm Oberst Fleury die Avantgarde, welchen 1 Offr., 20 Mann mit Axten, zur Wegräumung derer Pallisaden, vorgingen. Und auf dem linken Flügel bestand dieses Detachement aus 100 Freiwilligen unterm Major Steward mit 1 Offr., 20 Pioniers. Diese avancierten Detachements hatten nicht geladen. Um ½ 1 Uhr fing der Sturm an. Das Forth wurde ganz umringt, erstiegen, und ergab sich mit geringem Verlust auf der feindlichen Seite nach einem kurzen Gefecht.

Aus South Carolina erhielten wir Nachricht, dass der Gnl. Lincoln am 20 Juny den Oberst Maitland, der auf James Island mit dem 71 Rgmt., von Trumbach postiert war, angegriffen habe, durch das besondere Bravour dieser Trouppen aber zurück geschlagen worden. Lincoln machte den Angriff just zu der Zeit, da viele Soldaten zum Provisionsempfang abwesend waren, und war sehr hizzig in seiner Attaque.

*July 20*

Die Rangers, Legion und 17 Dragoner kamen heute von Verplancks Point zurück und lagerten sich auf dem rechten Flügel der Armee.

had not loaded their firearms.  At half past twelve the storming of the fort began.  It was completely surrounded, scaled, and surrendered after a short engagement with a small loss on the enemy side.

We received news from South Carolina that on 20 June General Lincoln[20] had attacked Colonel Maitland,[21] who was posted on James Island with the 71st and the Regiment von Trümbach, but he had been repulsed by the exceptional bravery of those troops.  Lincoln made the attack, which was very spirited, at the very time that many soldiers were absent to receive provisions.

*July 20*

The Rangers, Legion and 17th Dragoons came back today from Verplanck's Point and encamped on the army's right wing.

*July 21*

The Jäger Corps had to march from the left to the right wing of the army to cover its right flank and took post in a wood at Tuckahoe.

We received news today that Lord Cornwallis had arrived in New York from England in the frigate *Greyhound,* whereupon the army

*July 22*

marched back to Phillipse's House and into the former camp.

*July 21*

Das Jäger Corps musste vom linken auf den rechten Flügel der Armee marschieren, um deren rechte Flanque zu decken. Selbiges nahm seinen Posten in einem Walde zu Turkeyhoe.

Wir erhielten heute Nachricht, dass Lord Cornwallis in der *Greyhound* Fregatte von England in Newyork angekommen, worauf die Armee

*July 22*

in das vorherige Lager nach Philipshouse zurück marschierte.

*July 30*

Der Oberst von Wurmb mit denen berittenen und 150 Fuss Jägers machte heute eine Patrouille nach Terytown. Die Cavallerie stiess auf eine feindliche von 60 Pferden, welche ausriss und in Nachsezzen nur 1 Mann verlohr. Auch wurden 4 Mann von Emerichs Dragoner dem Feind wieder abgenommen, welche des Morgens in einem Scharmützel waren gefangen worden.

*July 31*

Heute früh marschierte die Armee nach Kingsbridge zurück. Die Rgmtr. und Corps bezogen eben die Emplacements, die sie vorher an diesem Ort gehabt hatten — das Jäger Corps also auch wieder auf dem Spitingdevil.

*August 1*

Ein englischer Capt. von einem Transport Schiff, der mit 38 Matrosen in einer Schloop von Boston aus der Gefangenschaft desertiert war, kam in Newyork an und brachte die

*July 30*

Colonel von Wurmb undertook a patrol today with the mounted and 150 foot jägers to Tarrytown. The cavalry fell in with an enemy patrol of sixty horse, who rode off and lost only one man in the pursuit. Four of Emmerich's dragoons, who had been captured during the morning in a skirmish, were also retaken from the enemy.

*July 31*

Early this morning the army marched back to Kingsbridge. The regiments and corps occupied precisely the positions which they had previously had there. Consequently the Jäger Corps was posted once again on Spuyten Duyvil.

***August 1***

An English captain of a transport ship, who had escaped from captivity with thirty-eight sailors in a sloop from Boston, arrived in New York and brought news that the the people of Boston had equipped a fleet to go to Penobscot to take the British post there, which had been recently established under Brig. Gen. McLean[22] for the purpose of protecting the ships timber which was to be felled. Commodore Sir George Collier[23] therefore put to sea with the *Raisonable,* the frigates *Greyhound, Blonde, Virginia, Galathea* and *Camilla,* and the sloop *Otter* to frustrate the enemy's designs.

N.B: See 9 September for the fortunate outcome of this enterprise.

Nachricht, dass die Bostonianer eine Flotte ausgerüstet, um nach Penobscot zu gehen, um den dasigen englischen Posten, der zum Schutz des zu hauenden Schiffe Bauholzes neuerdings alda unterm Br. Gl. McLean war etabliert worden, weg zu nehmen. Der Commodore Sir George Collier lief deswegen mit der *Raisonable* und denen Fregatten *Greyhound, Blonde, Virginia, Galathea, Camilla* und sloop *Otter* aus, um das Vorhaben des Feindes zu hintertreiben.

N.B: Der glückliche Erfolg dieses Vorhabens unterm 9 Sept.

*August 5*

Alarmierte eine feindliche Cavallerie Patrouille die Vorposten zu Hothams Heights und nahm in der Nachbarschaft der Legion einige Refugees gefangen. Die Legion, Rangers und auch die Jägers setzten solcher nach und ein Theil der Legion holte selbige jenseits Newrochelle ein, da sie 40 Mann Infanterie an sich gezogen hatte, welche ihr Feuer auf die Legion gaben und sich darauf zerstreuten, wodurch 2 Mann blieben und 7 blessiert wurden. Die Rangers und Jägers kamen zu spat.

*August 6*

In denen Festungswerken zu Laurel Hill wird jezzo mit besonderem Fleiss gearbeitet.

*August 10*

Erhielten wir Nachricht, dass Grenada und St. Vincent von denen Franzosen genommen worden, und dass am 6 July eine See Bataille zwischen Admiral Byron und Destaing vorgefallen, welche nicht entscheidend gewesen.

*August 18*

Dreissig Schiffe aus Georgien kamen in Newyork an, welche die Nachtricht mit bringen, dass die königl.

*August 5*

An enemy cavalry patrol turned out the advanced posts at Hotham's Heights and took prisoner some refugees in the Legion's neighbourhood. The Legion, Rangers, and the jägers too, set off in pursuit and part of the Legion overtook them beyond New Rochelle, for they had collected forty infantry, who fired on the Legion and then scattered. As a result two men were killed and seven wounded. The Rangers and jägers came too late.

*August 6*

In the fortifications at Laurel Hill work is now proceeding with exceptional industry.

*August 10*

We received news that Grenada and St. Vincent had been captured by the French and that on 6 July a sea battle between Admirals Byron and d'Estaing had taken place. It was not decisive.

*August 18*

Thirty ships arrived in New York from Georgia, bringing news that the royal troops were quartered partly at Beaufort and partly at Savannah during the summer heat.

*August 19*

Last night the enemy's Major Lee[24] stormed Paulus Hook with 400 men. He passed the ditch in front of the abatis, the abatis itself, and penentrated a work before the British were aware of it, taking them prisoner. A Hessian NCO, who with fifteen men formed the picket in a blockhouse,

Trouppen Theils zu Beauforth und Theils zu Savannah
während der Sommer Hizze einquartiert waren.

*August 19*

Der feindl. Major Lee stürmte verwichene Nacht mit 400
Mann Paulers Hook.  Er passierte den Graben vor dem
Verhau, den Verhau selbst und drang in ein Werk, ehe es
die Engländer gewahr wurden, nahm selbige auch
gefangen.  Ein hessischer Utr. Offr. mit 15 Mann, welcher
in einem Blockhaus das Picket hatte und auf den Lärmen
herauslief, um zu sehen was neues passierte, wurde mit
10 Mann gefangen.  Der Capt. Schaller aber mit 1 Offr.,
25 Hessen warf sich in eine kleine Redutte und fing den
Feind an zu beschiessen.  Er wurde zwar aufgefordert sich
su ergeben, behauptete aber seinen Posten.  Der Feind
retirierte sich darauf mit seinen Gefangenen (100 Mann)
nachdem er zuvor einige Barracken angesteckt hatte.  Ein
Batt. leichte Infanterie und Buskirkes Provincialen, welche
von Newyork über geschickt wurden, verfolgte ihn zwar
bis an die Newbridge, holten ihn aber nicht ein.

*August 26*

Lief der Vice Admiral Arbuthnot mit der ersten Division
der Kaufartheyflotte von England in Newyork ein.  Er hatte
das 80te und 81e neu errichtete Regmt., nebst denen
englischen Rekrutten, an board.

*September 2*

Durch das July Pacquet, so Falmouth den 7en July verliess,
erfahren wir die merkwürdige Nachricht, dass England
genötigt gewesen, denen Spaniern den Krieg zu declarieren
und dieses geschah auch heute in Newyork durch den
Governor Tryon mit denen gewöhnlichen Formalitäten,

ran out on hearing the din to see what was happening and was captured with ten of his men. Captain Schaller, however, threw himself with one officer and twenty-five Hessians into a small redoubt and commenced firing at the enemy. He was called upon to surrender but maintained his post. The enemy then retired with their prisoners (one hundred men) after first setting fire to some barracks. A battalion of light infantry and Buskirk's Provincials, who were sent over from New York, pursued them as far as New Bridge but did not overtake them.

## August 26

Vice Admiral Arbuthnot[25] put into New York with the first division of the merchant fleet from England. He had the newly raised 80th and 81st[26] Regiments on board, together with the British recruits.

## September 2

By the July packet, which left Falmouth on 7 July, we learn the remarkable news that England has been obliged to declare war on the Spaniards, and this was also done in New York today by Governor Tryon with the usual formalities.

## September 8

The 44th and the Regiments von Lossberg and von Knyphausen embarked to go to Canada.

## September 9

Sir George Collier's expedition against the New England fleet has turned out rather successfully. Sir George sailed

*September 8*

Das 44e Rgmt., Losberg u. Knyphausen embarquierten, um nach Canada zu gehen.

*September 9*

Sir George Colliers Expedition gegen die Neu Englische Flotte ist ziemlich glücklich aus gefallen. Sir George segelte am 2ten August mit seinem Geschwader von Sandy Hook und erreichte den Penobscot Fluss den 14teh frühe. Das feindl. Geschwader hatte schon seyt 3 Wochen den Br. Gl. McLean bloquiert und erwartete nichts weniger als eine englische Flotte. Anfangs schien es als ob sie sich defendieren wollten, retirierten sich aber statt dessen bald darauf den Fluss hinauf, nachdem sie ihre zur Bloquade an Land gehabten Soldaten an board genommen. Bey der Herannäherung der englischen Schiffe, steckten sie die ihrige in Brand und die Leute retirierten sich in die Wälder. Der Sloop *Hunter* von 18 und *Hampdon* von 20 Canonen fielen in englische Hände, ehe sie angesteckt werden konnten. Die übrigen, so verbrandten, waren 14 armierte Schiffe von 32 zu 16 Canonen und neben denen noch 24 Transport Schiffe, so dass also nicht ein einziges Schiff davon kam. Sir George hatte das gute Glück, die Brig *Nancy* von 16 und *Rover* von 10 Canonen in der See zu nehmen, welche vor der Flotte creuzten und dahero kam es, dass solche so vollkommen surprisiert wurde. Die Feinde mussten ihre Rückreise nach Boston durch die Wälder machen, welche mehrentheils unbewohnt und Wildnisse sind.

*September 10*

Heute wurde der Anfang gemacht, die Redutten auf Hothams Heights zu demolieren, in dem die neuen Linien zu Laurel Hill beynahe fertig sind. Solchergestalt werden in Zukunft

with his squadron from Sandy Hook on 2 August and reached the Penobscot River early on the 14th. The enemy squadron had already been blockading Brig. Gen. McLean for three weeks and the last thing they were expecting was a British fleet. It seemed at first as if they might be prepared to defend themselves, but instead they retired soon afterwards up the river, having taken on board the soldiers whom they had had on land for the blockade. On the approach of the British ships they set fire to their own and the men retired into the woods. The sloops *Hunter* of 18 guns and *Hampden* of 20 fell into the hands of the British before they could be set on fire. The rest, which were burnt in this manner, were fourteen armed ships from 32 to 16 guns and twenty-four transport ships as well. And so, not a single ship escaped. Sir George had the good fortune to capture at sea the brigs *Nancy* of 16 guns and *Rover* of 10, which were cruising ahead of the fleet, and this is the reason for its being so completely surprised. The enemy had to make their return journey to Boston through the woods, which are mostly uninhabited wildernesses.

### September 10

A start was made today on demolishing the redoubts on Hotham's Heights, for the new lines at Laurel Hill are almost ready. Thus the royal lines will in future be confined solely to York Island and be covered by Harlem Creek so as to be defended better and by fewer men.

### September 13

Colonel Tarleton[27] marched off from here this evening with the Legion cavalry and twenty mounted jägers to attack an enemy cavalry detachment at North Castle.

sich die königl. Linien bloss auf York Island einschränken und von der Harlem Creek gedeckt werden, mithin besser und durch weniger Menschen zu vertheidigen sein.

*September 13*

Der Oberst Tarleton mit der Cavallerie der Legion und 20 berittenen Jägers marschierte diesen Abend von hier ab, um ein feindliches Cavallerie Detachement zu North Castle zu attaquieren. Er kam den nächsten Morgen früh alda an und fand, dass der Feind sich schon retiriert hatte, machte aber noch einige Gefangene von einem auseinander gesprengten Piquet. In zurück Marsch wurde er von der Cavallerie des Oberst White und der Miliz verfolgt und verlohr 8 Mann.

*September 16*

Das 64e Rgmt. verliess heute seinen Posten zu Verplancks Point und ging nach Newyork ab.

Folgende Rgmtr. erhielten Ordre sich zum Embarquement parat zu halten: alle Grenadiers, 200 jägers, leichte Infanterie, Rangers, 7, 23, 33, 37, 54 und 57 nebst Fannings Corps, um, wie man vermuthet, nach Süden zu gehen. Auch brachte ein Express Boot von General Dalling von Jamaica die Nachricht, dass die Franzosen diese Insul mit einem Angriff droheten, und dass es an Trouppen zu deren Vertheidigung fehle.

*September 17*

Lord Cornwallis wurde mit denen 7, 23, 33 u. 57 Rgmt., Queens Rangers und Irish Volunteers embarquiert, um nach Jamaica zu gehen.

He arrived there early next morning and found that the enemy had already retired, but he still captured some members of a dispersed picket. On the return march he was pursued by Colonel White's cavalry[28] and the militia and lost eight men.

### September 16

Today the 64th Regiment left its post at Verplanck's Point and went off to New York.

The following regiments received orders to hold themselves in readiness for embarkation: all the Grenadiers, 200 jägers, light infantry, Rangers, 7th, 23rd, 33rd, 37th, 54th and 57th, together with Fanning's Corps, presumably to go to the south. An express boat from General Dalling brought news from Jamaica that the French were threatening the island with an attack and that there was a shortage of troops for its defence.

### September 17

Lord Cornwallis embarked with the 7th, 23rd, 33rd and 57th Regiments, the Queen's Rangers and Irish Volunteers to go to Jamaica.

### September 18

All posts beyond Kingsbridge were withdrawn today except the Jäger Corps, which remained completely alone to occupy Spuyten Duyvil. We were therefore very exposed and lay completely cut off from the army. Most of the night we were under arms.

*September 18*

Alle Posten jenseits Kingsbridge wurden heute eingezogen, nur das Jäger Corps blieb ganz allein stehen, um den Spitingdevil zu besezzen. Wir waren dadurch sehr exponiert und lagen ganz von der Armee abgeschnitten. Die grösste Zeit des Nachts standen wir unterm Gewehr.

*September 19*

Die Legion marschierte heute nach Oyster Bay auf Longisland, um diese Insul für denen häufigen Plünderungen derer über den Sund kommenden New Engländer zu schüzzen.

*September 20*

Das 64e Rgmt. rückte hinter dem Jäger Corps ins Lager, um solches in Nothfall unterstützen zu können.

*September 21*

Commodore Hammond mit der 2en Division derer engl. Kaufmanns Flotte kam zu Newyork an. Er hatte die hessische Recroutten an board.

*September 23*

Die Recroutten wurden debarquiert und zu ihren respec. Rgmtrn. geschickt. Das Jäger Corps erhielt 2 Offrs. und 230 Mann.

*September 24*

Lord Cornwallis ging heute in See.

*September 28*

Ein spanisches Schiff war durch einen englischen Kaper gefangen und in dessen Logg-Buch fand sich, dass es die franz. Flotte am 31 August an denen grossen Bahama Banks

*September 19*

Today the Legion marched to Oyster Bay on Long Island to protect that island from frequent plundering by the New Englanders coming across the sound.

*September 20*

The 64th Regiment moved into camp behind the Jäger Corps to be in readiness to support it in an emergency.

*September 21*

Commodore Hamond arrived at New York with the second division of the British merchant fleet. He had the Hessian recruits on board.

*September 23*

The recruits were disembarked and sent to their respective regiments. The Jäger Corps received two officers and 230 men.

*September 24*

Lord Cornwallis put to sea.

*September 28*

A Spanish ship was captured by a British privateer and it was discovered in its log book that it had sighted the French fleet on 31 August on a westerly course off the Grand Bahama Banks. This caused Lord Cornwallis to be recalled and measures to be taken to protect us in New York, for Jamaica would thus be out of danger and New

unter einem westlichen Cours gesehen. Dieses veranlasste, das Lord Cornwallis zurück gerufen und Anstalt gemacht wurden, uns in Newyork zu vertheidigen, weilen Jamaica solcher Gestalt ausser Gefahr sey und wahrscheinlicher Weise Newyork der Gegenstand der Flotte sein müsse. Lord Cornwallis retournierte auch

**September 29**

nach Sandyhook, worauf dessen Trouppen debarquiert und zur Deckung derer Narrows und des Landungs Platzes zu Denyses House placiert worden.

**September 30**

Ein Detachement von 100 Jägers unterm Capt. v. Wangenheim marschierte nach Laurel Hill, um in der verlassenen Lager des Rgmts. v. Bose Posto zu fassen, welches nach Newyork beordert war.

**October 3**

Eine Patrouille des Jäger Corps traff diesen Morgen eine feindliche zu East Chester an und nahm den Offr. mit dem Trompeter davon gefangen.

**October 4**

Von denen Trouppen, welche am 8 Sept. nach Canada gesegelt, kamen einige Schiffe mit der traurigen Nachricht wieder zurück, dass sie in einem Sturme zerstreuet und einige davon (welche wusste man nicht gewiss) gescheitert wären. Es fand sich nachher, dass das gescheiterte ein Theil des Rgmts. v. Losberg an board gehabt und ein anderes, so den Major Stein mit einem Theil des Rgmts. von Knyphausen aufgehabt, wurde vom Feind, nachdem

York probably had to be the objective of the fleet. Lord Cornwallis returned

*September 29*

to Sandy Hook, whereupon his troops were disembarked and stationed to cover the Narrows and the landing place at Denys's House.

*September 30*

A detachment of one hundred jägers under Captain von Wangenheim marched to Laurel Hill to take post in the deserted camp of the Regiment von Bose, which had been ordered to New York.

*October 3*

This morning a patrol of the Jäger Corps fell in with one of the enemy's at Eastchester and captured its officer and bugler.

*October 4*

With regard to the troops who had sailed to Canada on 8 September, a few ships returned with the sad news that they had been scattered in a storm and some of them (it was not known for certain which) had foundered. It was discovered later that the one which had foundered had had part of the Regiment von Lossberg on board. Another, which had Major Stein on board with part of the Regiment von Knyphausen, was captured by the enemy, and its men were saved, after it had lost all its masts and was a total wreck.

According to reports the enemy has taken possession of Thunder Mountain[29] (a height not far from Stoney Point)

solches alle seine Maste verlohren und ein völliges Wrack war, gefangen und die Leute davon gerettet.

Nachrichten zufolge hat der Feind Besitz von der Thunder Barracks (eine Höhe nicht weit von Stoney Point) genommen und die Brigade des Gen. Maj. Howe ist bis North Castle vorgerückt.

### October 15

Die franz. Flotte liess sich am 6 Sept. bey Clarlestown sehen, ging aber sogleich wieder in See. Admiral Byron hat dem Admiral Parker das Commando der Flotte übergeben, weil er nach England geht. Zur Zeit als die Franzosen aus West Indien segelten, hatte man für sicher behauptet, dass solche nach Jamaica gegangen waren.

### October 20

Die franz. Flotte erschien auf Tybee und debarquierte die an board habenden Trouppen, welche sich mit der feindl. Armee unterm General Lincoln conjugierten und sofort nach Savannah marschierten, um den General Prevost zu belagern, während dem ihn die Flotte zu Wasser bloquierte. Das engl. Kriegs Schiff *Experiment* war bereits nebst einem anderen genommen, und da Savannah wenig befestigt und ein Theil der Engländer in Beauforth unterm Oberst Maidland standen, die nicht zum General Prevost stossen konnten, so war man für das Schicksal dieses Generals sehr besorgt, zumalen da ihm von hier aus nicht die geringste Assistance gegeben werden konnte, weilen wir keine Kriegs Flotte hier hatten.

Der General Washington orderte seine schwere Artillerie nach West Point und liess 4,000 Miliz unters Gewehr tretten, um auf alle Fälle mit der französischen Flotte, auch

and Maj. Gen. Howe's brigade has advanced to North Castle.

## October 15

The French fleet was sighted off Charlestown on 6 September but immediately put to sea again. As he is going to England, Admiral Byron has handed over command of the fleet to Admiral Parker. At the time that the French sailed from the West Indies it was said for certain that they had gone to Jamaica.

## October 20

The French fleet appeared off Tybee and disembarked the troops they had on board. These joined up with the enemy army under General Lincoln and marched at once to Savannah to besiege General Prevost, while the fleet blockaded him by sea. The British ship of war *Experiment*, and another one too, had already been captured. As Savannah was poorly fortified and part of the British, who were stationed under Colonel Maitland at Beaufort, could not join General Prevost, we were very worried about the general's fate, especially as he could not be afforded the slightest assistance from here, for here we had no fleet of warships.

General Washington ordered his heavy artillery to West Point and had 4,000 militia take up arms so as to be in readiness to co-operate in every eventuality with the French fleet and also against the army here. General Sullivan, who had been detached against the Indians, had returned and considerably reinforced the enemy army.

Work is proceeding with tireless activity on the fortification works at New York so as to be able to defend the army

gegen die hiesige Armee, co-operieren zu können. Der General Sullivan, so gegen die Indianer detachiert gewesen, war auch zurück gekommen und hatte die feindliche Armee um ein Ansehnliches verstärkt.

An denen Festungswerken zu Newyork wird mit unermüdeten Fleiss gearbeitet, um die Armee darinnen defendieren zu können, falls die Franzosen solche mit ihrer Flotte attaquieren wollten.

*October 21*

Stoney Point wurde diesen Abend abandoniert und die dasige Garnison ging nach Newyork.

*October 26*

Die Trouppen von Rhodeisland kamen zu Newyork an, welche Insul gleichfalls gänzlich verlassen war.

Die Nachrichten aus England sagen, dass die französische und spanische Flotte sich vereinigt, der englischen weit an der Anzahl Schiffe überlegen, und Plymouth vom 20ten bis 24ten August bloquiert gehabt, aber den Hafen dennoch attaquiert hatten.

*November 6*

Ein feindliches Detachement von 500 Pferdten unterm Oberst White allarmierte diesen Morgen das Jäger Corps, liess sich aber auf sonst nichts ein.

*November 7*

Die Armee bezog das ihr angewiesene Winterquartier auf York-, Long- und Staatenisland. Das Jäger Corps musste in

in them in case the French should choose to attack with their fleet.

*October 21*

Stoney Point was abandoned this evening and the garrison went to New York.

*October 26*

The troops from Rhode Island, which had also been completely abandoned, arrived at New York.

The reports from England say that the French and Spanish fleets have combined and are numerically far superior in ships to the British. They blockaded Plymouth from 20 to 24 August but had not yet attacked the port.

*November 6*

This morning an enemy detachment of 500 horse under Colonel White turned out the Jäger Corps but did not venture upon anything else.

*November 7*

The army moved into the winter quarters allotted to it on York, Long and Staten Islands. The Jäger Corps had to quarter themselves on Laurel Hill in huts which they had to build for themselves. The enemy army was still kept in the field in expectation of the French fleet.

*November 19*

Contrary to all expectations we received today the agreeable news that the siege of Savannah had been raised and the French had returned to the West Indies:

Hütten auf Laurel Hill cantonnieren, die es sich selbst erbauen musste. Die feindl. Armee hielt sich noch immer im Felde in Erwartung der französischen Flotte.

*November 19*

Gegen alle Erwartung erhielten wir heute die angenehme Nachricht, dass die Belagerung von Savannah aufgehoben und die Franzosen wieder nach denen West Indien zurück gegangen:

General Prevost gab sich alle Mühe die Stadt Savannah aufs äusserste zu vertheidigen und solche womöglich zu erhalten. Er liess deswegen viele neue Werke durch den Major Moncrief anlegen und fand sich bey dem Anrücken des Feindes schon einiger Massen in Vertheidigungs Stand. Colonel Maidland hatte sich auch durch undurchdringliche Moräste und Sümpfe gearbeitet und kam mit seinem Detachement ganz unvermuthet in Savannah an. Der Comte d'Estaing fing eine regelmässige Belagerung an und forderte den General Prevost zu verschiedenen Malen auf, sich denen Waffen des Königs von Frankreich zu ergeben, allein er gab ihm kein Gehör, ohngeachtet er die Stadt sehr cannonierte. D'Estaing wurde endlich unruhig, dass die engl. Flotte in West Indien allein sey, wollte dahero auch nicht länger mit den weiteren und langweiligen Approchieren abgeben, sondern stürmte die Werke den 11en Novbr. mit anbrechendem Tage, wurde aber zurück geschlagen, er selbst blessiert und Pulewsky, der 2ten Rebellen general, wurde todtgeschossen. Der Feind zog sich darauf zurück, re-embarquierte seine Artillerie, und hob die Belagerung nach einigen Tagen gänzlich auf. D'Estaing segelte nach West Indien und Gen. Lincoln marschierte mit denen Rebellen nach Charlestown.

Der wackere Oberst Maidland hatte sich auf seinem so fatiguen Marsch so entkräftet, dass er einige Tage nach

General Prevost made every effort to defend the town of Savannah to the last extremity and to hold it if possible. So he had many new works laid down by Major Moncrief[30] and on the approach of the enemy he was already in a fair state of defence. Colonel Maitland had also worked his way through impenetrable morasses and swamps and arrived in Savannah quite unexpectedly with his detachment. Comte d'Estaing embarked upon a regular siege and several times summoned General Prevost to surrender to the arms of the King of France, but he paid him no heed, notwithstanding that he severely cannonaded the town. At length d'Estaing became uneasy that the British fleet was alone in the West Indies. For this reason he was no longer prepared to bother with further tedious approaches and on 11 November[31] he stormed the works at dawn. He was, however, repulsed, he himself was wounded, and Pulaski,[32] the second rebel general, was shot dead. The enemy then withdrew, re-embarked their artillery, and raised the siege completely after a few days. D'Estaing sailed to the West Indies and General Lincoln marched with the rebels to Charlestown.

Brave Colonel Maitland had so weakened himself on so tiring a march that he fell victim to a fever a few days after his arrival in Savannah and died. The royal losses were not substantial.

### November 21

The army moved out this evening and fired a *feu de joie* on account of the failure of the French in the siege of Savannah.

General Washington's army was quartered at Morristown.

seiner Ankunft in Savannah in ein Fieber verfiel und starb. Der königl. Verlust war nicht beträchtlich.

*November 21*

Die Armee rückte diesen Abend aus und machte ein Freudenfeuer über die misslungene Belagerung derer Franzosen zu Savannah.

General Washington hatte seine Armee zu Morristown einquartiert.

*December 19*

General Clinton sah sich nunmehro im Stande, seine Operationen in denen südlichen Provincen fort zu sezzen, zu welchem Ende er heute mit folgenden Trouppen embarquiert worden:

> englische Grenadiers, leichte Infanterie, 7, 23, 33, 42, 63, 64 Rgmt., 250 Jägers (unterm Major Wurmb), hessische Grenadiers, Rgmt. v. Huyne, ein Detachement Chasseurs, 1 Bat. des 71 Rgmts., Fergusons Corps, Legion, und Newyork Volunteers.

*December 24*

Segelten obige Trouppen nach Sandyhook, bestehend in 80 Schiffen und unter Bedeckung von 5 Linien Schiffen und 5 Fregatten. Gen. Lt. v. Knyphausen cmdrt nunmehro Newyork und die davon abhängenden Posten.

∞ —— ∞

*December 19*

General Clinton now considered himself in a position to pursue his operations in the southern provinces. To this end he embarked today with the following troops:

> British Grenadiers, light infantry, 7th, 23rd, 33rd, 42nd,[33] 63rd, 64th Regiments, 250 jägers (under Major von Wurmb), Hessian Grenadiers, Regiment von Huyne, a detachment of chasseurs,[34] a battalion of the 71st Regiment,[35] Ferguson's Corps, Legion, and New York Volunteers.[36]

*December 24*

The above troops sailed to Sandy Hook in a fleet of eighty ships escorted by five ships of the line and five frigates. Lt. Gen. von Knyphausen is now in command of New York and the posts dependent on it.

# NOTES

## ∞ 1777 ∞

1.   Fort Flagstaff on Staten Island was built by the revolutionaries in June 1776 and captured by the British one month later.   It stood on Signal Hill at The Narrows.   Demolished in 1806, it was replaced by what became Fort Wadsworth, the site of which is now part of the Gateway National Recreation Area.

2.   Born in Blackheath, Kent, Andrew Snape Hamond (1738-1828) entered the Royal Navy in 1753 and saw service during the Seven Years' War, taking part as a lieutenant in the Battle of Quiberon Bay.   In July 1775, by then a captain, he was appointed to the *Roebuck*, newly launched at Chatham, and came out to the North American station, where he served till 1780.   Of particular note was his distinguished part in the siege of Charlestown.   He later became Lt. Governor of Nova Scotia, an MP, and Controller of the Navy Board for ten years.   Having previously been knighted, he was created a baronet in 1783.

3.   Milford Haven.

4.   Gwynn's Island lies at the mouth of the Piankatank River.

5.   Smith's Point is the southern headland at the mouth of the Potomac River.

6.   Cedar Point is the southern headland at the mouth of the Patuxent River.

7.   Ward's and Sharp's Islands lie at the mouth of the Choptank River.

8.   Bodkin's Point is the southern headland at the mouth of the Patapsco River.

9.   Montresor's journal gives the time as 9.30 a.m., which is almost certainly a mistranscription of 3.30 a.m. (John Montresor,

"Journals", *Collections of the New-York Historical Society for the Year 1881)*

10.    James Grant (1720-1806), the Laird of Ballindalloch in Banff, had taken part in the American theatre of the Seven Years' War and developed a contempt for the fighting qualities of the American soldier. While reconnoitring Fort Duquesne, he was captured but soon exchanged.    From 1763 to 1771 he went on to serve as Governor of East Florida.    According to Alden, "he was sensible, able, industrious, relatively good-humoured, and hospitable.  He invested money of his own ... and he encouraged the ventures of others."  Relinquishing his office due to illness, he returned home and became an MP before going out to America again as a major general in 1775.  He was then involved in the New York campaign and the brief occupation of New Jersey.  Now taking part in the Philadelphia campaign, he would later be dispatched to the West Indies, where he led a successful expedition to capture St. Lucia. He departed for England in August 1779 but his disposition of the troops formed the basis for British successes in the Caribbean during the closing years of the war.  He remained an MP for many years and was promoted to full general in 1796.  (Mark Mayo Boatner III, *Encyclopedia of the American Revolution* (D. McKay Co., 1966); John R. Alden, *The South in the Revolution 1763-1789* (Baton Rouge: Louisiana State University Press, 1957).

11.    "skirmishers": a translation of "Blänkers", a word found in no German dictionary.  A clue to its meaning may nevertheless be gained from the *Oxford English Dictionary*, where there is an archaic but related word of Germanic origin:

> "Blencher (or Blancher): A person or thing employed to turn or frighten away, eg a scarecrow; in hunting, one placed to turn the deer from going in particular directions."

The German and English words have clearly diverged some-what in meaning, but the indication is clearly there that "Blänkers" was a jäger expression applied to military use and having the meaning assigned to it here.  If the men had not been ahead but to the side, an appropriate translation would have been "flankers".

12.  "in General Orders": a translation of "bey der Parole". The reading of the password immediately preceded General Orders.

13.  For corroboration of most of this paragraph, see Colonel George Hanger, *A Letter to the Right Hon. Lord Castlereagh* (London, 1808), 83. Hanger served in the Jäger Corps.

14.  "British chasseurs": a reference to Ferguson's Corps armed with his breech-loading rifles.

15.  Born in 1752, William Scott was captain of the light infantry company of the 17th Regiment (*Army Lists*).

16.  "line": a translation of an archaic meaning of "Treffen". Today it means "action, encounter, or battle".

17.  "bugle-horn" was the expression used in the British Army to refer to what, as here, the Hessian forces called a "Halbmond", literally, a "crescent".

18.  Charles Grey (1729-1807) earned the sobriquet "No Flint" Grey for the surprise attack mentioned here, an action which he later repeated with equal success at Paoli and New Tappan. Entering the British Army as an ensign in 1748, he had seen service in the Seven Years' War, first as a captain at the Battle of Minden, where he was wounded, and second as Lt. Colonel of the 98th Regiment at the capture of Havana. Coming out to America as a major general in 1776, he displayed a vigour and activity in which many other leading officers were wanting. At the Battle of Germantown he commanded the 3rd Brigade and in autumn 1778 he inflicted heavy losses on the enemy by the capture and destruction of stores at New Bedford and Martha's Vineyard. In later life, as the long war with France began, he would see distinguished service as a lt. general in Flanders and the West Indies. Promoted to full general in 1794, he became a privy councillor and in 1806 was advanced to the dignities of Viscount Howick and Earl Grey, having been created a Baron five years earlier. (*Dictionary of National Biography* (London, 1885-1900, vol. 23); Boatner, *Encyclopedia*)

19.  The reference to Chadd's Ford, which is clearly misplaced, is puzzling. Other sources say that the British army crossed at

Fat Land Ford. According to Baurmeister, von Wreden's diversion took place at Gordon's Ford (Carl Baurmeister, *Revolution in America.* translated by Berbhard A. Uhlendorf (Rutgers University Press, 1957), 116, note 52). If so, the Journal of the Jäger Corps appears to have misnamed and confused the ford where the diversion took place with the ford where the army crossed, transposing the two.

20. "Rangers": a common abbreviation in this journal for the Queens Rangers, a British American corps — part cavalry, part infantry — commanded by Lt. Colonel John Graves Simcoe.

21. "1st Battalion light infantry": apparently a slip of the pen for the 2nd Battalion. It is most unlikely that the 1st Battalion formed the advanced corps of both the right wing and the centre.

22. "500 rods": 2,750 yards.

23. *chevaux de frise*: submerged frames containing projecting long iron or wooden spikes.

24. The youngest son of a baronet, Thomas Musgrave (1738-1812) had served in the 3rd Regiment (the Buffs) at the capture of Guadeloupe in May 1759. As Lt. Colonel of the 40th Regiment he distinguished himself, as stated here, at the Battle of Germantown by throwing himself and 200 of his men into the Chew House and holding up the enemy's advance. He went on to serve in the West Indies and as the last British Commandant of New York. In later life he served indifferently under Cornwallis in India for some three years before retiring to England and commanding for a time the Northern District. In 1800 he inherited the baronetcy. He died a full general at his London home in Bolton Street, Piccadilly, and was buried at St. George's, Hanover Square. (*ODNB*)

25. Brigadier James Tanner Agnew (1719-1777) was killed by a sniper, Hans Boyer, while leading his brigade. He is buried in the De Benneville Family Burial Grounds, Philadelphia.

26. The raid was in fact commanded by Maj. Gen. John Sullivan of the Continental Army.

27.   Born in Strachur, Scotland, John Campbell (*c.* 1725-1806) had entered the British Army as a lieutenant in Loudoun's Highlanders in 1745 and helped put down the Jacobite Rebellion. Having served in Flanders in 1747, he took part in the Seven Years' War, being wounded at Ticonderoga in 1758 as a captain in the 42nd Highlanders, and being involved in the expeditions against Martinico and Havana four years later, when, as a lt.colonel, he commanded the 17th Regiment.   Appointed lt. colonel of the 57th Regiment in 1773, he came out with it to America in 1776 and for the next two years was stationed at New York, where, with the local rank of brigadier general, he commanded at Staten Island.   Late in 1778 he was detached by Clinton to take command in West Florida and in February 1779 was promoted to the regular rank of major general.   Left out on a limb at Pensacola, he capitulated in May 1781 to the Spanish in the face of overwhelming odds, having put up a stout defence of the town. (*Army Lists; Appletons' Cyclopædia of American Biography* (New York, 1888-  ); Boatner, *Encyclopedia*)

28.   A Rhode Islander, Colonel Christopher Greene was a Continental officer who had been captured at Quebec before being exchanged.   For the defence of Red Bank he received the thanks of Congress, which presented him with an elegant sword. On 14 May 1781 he was killed by De Lancey's troops in Westchester County, New York. (Francis B. Heitman, *Historical Register of Officers of the Continental Army during the War of the Revolution* (Reprint, Clearfield Publishing Co. Inc., 2000))

29.   Hotham has not been identified.   He does not appear in David Syrett and R. L. DiNardo eds, *The Commissioned Sea Officers of the Royal Navy 1660-1815* (Navy Records Society, 1994).

30.   Major General the Hon. John Vaughan, a younger son of the 3rd Viscount Lisburne, had come out to America in 1776, leading the Grenadiers in the Battle of Long Island and taking part in the Battle of White Plains, where he was wounded in the thigh.   On returning to England in 1779, he was appointed Commander-in-Chief in the Leeward Islands. Having arrived at Barbados in February 1780, he managed to reinforce St. Lucia, by concentrating troops from Antigua and St. Kitts, in time to abort

with the navy an attempt by de Guichen to recapture the island on 23 March. (*DNB*; Sir John Fortescue, *A History of the Brtish Army*, vol. III (Macmillan & Co. Ltd., 1902), 334-6; Alan Valentine, *The British Establishment, 1760-1784*, vol II (University of Oklahoma Press, 1970), 886)

31.  Sir James Wallace (1731-1803) entered the Royal Naval Academy in 1746 and was promted to captain on 10 January 1771. He died an admiral of the blue. (Syrett and DiNardo eds, *The Commissioned Sea Officers*)

32.  Maj. Gen. Sir Thomas Spencer Wilson Bt of Uckfield, Sussex, came out to America in 1777 and would undertake no distinguished service. He died a full general.

33.  "Greene": Maj. Gen. Nathanael Greene (1742-1786). As GOC in the south he would excel in the campaigns there of 1781 and 1782.

# ∞ 1778 ∞

1.  On 14 April, according to Montresor and Baurmeister.

2.  According to Montresor and Serle, the resolves of Congress became known in Philadelphia on 27 April.

3.  According to Baurmeister, the revolutionaries fired a *feu de joie* on 2 May to celebrate the recognition of American independence by France and Spain. On 6 and 7 May Montresor records that revolutionary newspaper reports had reached Philadelphia.

4.  A younger son of the Earl of Leven and Melville, the Hon. Alexander Leslie (1731-1794) had entered the British Army in 1753 as an ensign in the 3rd Regiment of Foot Guards (the Scots Guards). By 1768 he had risen to the lt. colonelcy of the 64th Regiment stationed at Boston. In 1776 he played a prominent part as a brigadier general in the New York campaign and in 1780 accompanied Clinton to the south, having been promoted to the local rank of major general. On conclusion of the

Charlestown campaign he went back with Clinton to New York, only to return to Charlestown in December 1780 to reinforce Cornwallis and take part in the disastrous winter campaign in North Carolina. In late July 1781, while at Portsmouth, Virginia, he was appointed by Cornwallis to command at Charlestown and at the same time was notified of his promotion to the local rank of lt. general. He did not sail to Charlestown directly but called first at New York, where he took part in the councils of war convened in response to the developing crisis in Virginia. He did not reach Charlestown until November. With the fate of the war decided, he proceeded to evacuate the town and Savannah in 1782, a year in which he was promoted to the regular rank of major general. Leslie's end came at Beechwood House about three miles west of Edinburgh. As second in command in Scotland, he had been involved in suppressing a mutiny among fencible troops at Glasgow, where he was knocked down by a missile thrown by a riotous mob. On his way back to headquarters he became dangerously ill and died on 27 December 1794. He is buried in Jedburgh Abbey. A portrait of him by Gainsborough is in a private collection surveyed by the Scottish National Portrait Gallery in 1964. (Boatner, *Encyclopedia*; Ian Saberton ed., *The Cornwallis Papers: The Campaigns of 1780 and 1781 in the Southern Theatre of the American Revolutionary War* (The Naval & Military Press Ltd., 2010); John Kay, *A Series of Portraits and Caricature Etchings ... With Biographical Sketches and Illustrative Anecdotes* (Edinburgh, 1838); *Army Lists*)

5.   23rd": other sources say the regiment was the 20th.

6.   Vice Admiral John "Foul-weather Jack" Byron (1723-1786) would serve only briefly as the naval commander-in-chief on the North American station.

7.   Major John Butler (1728-1796) was Deputy Superintendent of Indian Affairs north of the Ohio. Based in Niagara, he led a raid on Wyoming Valley in July 1778 and completely destroyed it.

8.   Although, as we have read, his raid on Staten Island was a failure, Maj. Gen. John Sullivan (1740-1795) was considered by

Washington as one of his most valuable generals, taking part in the victory at Trenton and the Battles of Brandywine and Germantown. He went on to besiege Newport, Rhode Island, but abandoned the affair shortly after the departure of d'Estaing and the French fleet for Boston. In 1779 he led a successful expedition against the Iroquois, which so impaired his health that he resigned, whereupon he was promptly elected to Congress. From 1785 to 1790 he would serve as Governor of New Hampshire. (Boatner, *Encyclopedia*)

9. "Legion": a uniform abbreviation in this journal for the British Legion, a British American corps — part cavalry, part infantry — commanded by Lt. Colonel Banastre Tarleton.

10. Now part of Plymouth, Connecticut.

11. According to von Krafft, the date of this incident was 11 October. (Johann Carl Philip von Krafft, "Journal", *Collections of the New-York Historical Society for the Year 1782*)

## ∞ 1779 ∞

1. Zwieback: a rusk or biscuit made by baking a small loaf and then toasting slices till they become dry and crisp.

2. Rear Admiral Samuel Barrington (1729-1800) was the fourth son of the 1st Viscount Barrington of Beckett Hall, Shrivenham, Oxforshire. In 1778 he was appointed naval commandeer-in-chief on the Leeward Islands station.

3. Besides distinguishing himself in the capture of St. Lucia, Maj. Gen William Medows (1738-1813) saw action in North America (where he took part in the Battle of Brandywine), the Cape of Good Hope, and India, where he also became Governor of Bombay and then of Madras. In 1793 he was made a Knight of the Bath and would die a full general.

4. Archibald Campbell (1739-1791), Lt. Colonel of the 2nd Battalion, 71st (Highland) Regiment, had led the expedition

which captured Savannah in late December 1778. After Augustine Prevost assumed overall command on joining him with a force from East Florida, he returned on leave to England.

5. Maj. Gen. Robert Howe (1732-1786) was the Contninetal officer commanding in the Southern Department. He had attempted an invasion of East Florida, but it failed as a result of hunger, sickness, and insubordination.

6. Brig. Gen. Edward Mathew occupied Portsmouth in May 1779 during the highly successful expedition to Virginia commanded by himself and Sir George Collier. He had come out to America in command of a brigade of Guards and had taken part in the New York campaign. Promoted to major general, he saw action at Springfield, New Jersey, in June 1780 before returning to England not long after. He died a full general.

7. Maj. Gen. William Erskine had commanded a brigade in the Battle of Long Island, was Tryon's second in command in 1779 during the Connecticut Coast Raid, and currently occupied the post of Quartermaster General. He would soon return to England. He became a lt. general in 1787 and was created a baronet in 1791. (Boatner, *Encyclopedia*)

8. Verdrietige Hook, the location of Stoney Point on the west bank of the Hudson, is the name by which Hook Mountain was known to the first Dutch settlers. It means "Tedious Point", a reference perhaps to the time it remained in view when sailing past, or possibly to the troublesome winds encountered by sailors in its vicinity. Tallers Point, the spit of land projecting opposite from the east bank of the Hudson, was the location of Fort Lafayette (otherwise known as Verplanck's Point). Between it and the Hook lay Kings Ferry.

9. Brig. Gen. James Paterson, as he signed his surname, did not highly distinguish himself in America. Soon he would be appointed by Clinton to be Commandant of Charlestown, South Carolina, but overwhelmed by the confusion, perplexity and civil nature of the business, he was not up to the job, finding

himself "embarked on a situation out of the line of my profession." Fortunately he soon fell ill and was conveniently shipped to New York for the recovery of his health. Promoted to major general in 1782, he commanded British land forces in Nova Scotia after the war. At times his name is misspelt by historians. (Saberton ed., *The Cornwallis Papers*, vol. I; Benjamin Franklin Stevens, *The Campaign in Virginia: the Clinton Cornwallis Controversity* (London, 1887-8), vol. II, 449; WO 65/164(1) (UK National Archives, Kew))

10. Maj. Gen. Horatio Gates (1728-1806), the hero of Saratoga, who would be abjectly defeated in the Battle of Camden.

11. Thomas Thomas (*c.* 1744-1824) was Colonel of the 2nd Regiment of the Westchester revolutionary militia. In November 1778 he was captured by the Queen's Rangers at his house. He escaped from captivity on Long Island by breaking his parole and continued serving as a militia officer till the end of the war.

12. Born in Switzerland, Maj. Gen. Augustine Prevost (1723-1786) was commander of British forces in East Florida. He had now moved north and after the capture of Savannah in December 1778 he assumed overall command. Highlights of his outstanding performace were his victory at Briar Creek in March 1779, his attempt to capture Charlestown, and his successful defence of Savannah when besieged by the French and revolutionaries in the autumn. In the summer of 1780 he returned to England, having served twenty-two years in North America and the West Indies. (Boatner, *Encyclopedia*; Saberton ed., *The Cornwallis Papers*)

13. Lt. Colonel Henry Johnson (1748-1835) was Lt. Colonel of the 17th Regiment and would be captured with the garrison of Stoney Point by a *coup de main* on 16 July 1779. He would be created a baronet in 1818 and died a full general.

14. The son of Dr. Alexander Webster, an eminent clergyman of Edinburgh, James Webster (*c.* 1743-1781) was Lt. Colonel of the 33rd Regiment, a Yorkshire regiment of which Cornwallis was Colonel. Having been involved in the New Jersey and Philadelphia campaigns and the occupation of Verplanck's

Point, he would play a distinguished part in southern operations, notably commanding the British right wing in the Battle of Camden and the British left wing in the Battle of Guilford, an action in which he was mortally wounded.  Esteemed on both sides of the political divide for his high character and talents, he was described by an adversary as uniting to consummate skill and intrepidity "a generous forbearance and humanity towards such of his enemies as fell within the influence of his power, as secured their gratitude and most exalted admiration."  (Stevens, *Clinton-Cornwallis Controversy*, ii, 463; Fortescue, *British Army*, iii, 213; Alexander Garden Jr., *Anecdotes of the Revolutionary War* (Charleston, 1822), 280-2; Saberton ed., *The Cornwallis Papers*)

15.    In August 1777 Captain Andreas Emmerich, an experienced German officer, was authorised to raise a company of riflemen from the British American regiments.  Having proved its effectiveness two months later during Clinton's foray into the Highlands, it was expanded in 1778 to a corps — part infantry, part cavalry — and Emmerich was promoted to lt. colonel.  From then onwards things began to go downhill and due to unrest and insubordination the corps was disbanded in August 1779.

16.    Having seen service in the American theatre of the Seven Years' War, Thomas Stirling (1731-1808) returned to America in 1776 as Lt. Colonel of the 42nd (Highland) Regiment and took part in the New York and New Jersey campaigns.  By now a brigadier general, he was severely wounded in the thigh during the Springfield foray in June 1780.  Succeeding his brother as Baronet of Ardoch in 1799, he died a full general.

17.    Brig. Gen. "Mad Anthony" Wayne (1745-1796).

18.    A French nobleman, François-Louis Teissedre de Fleury was a Colonel in the revolutionary Corps of Engineers.  He had seen much distinguished service, taking part, *inter alia*, in the Battles of Brandywine, Germantown, and Monmouth.  Later he would serve in the siege of Yorktown.  For his bravery in the assault on Stoney Point Congress would award silver medals not only to him but also to Wayne and Stewart, the first of only eleven awarded during the Revolutionary War.

19.   Born in Anne Arundel County, Maryland, Major John Stewart (1753-1783) would be promoted on 10 February 1781 to lt. colonel and see service in the Carolinas.  He was killed by a fall from his horse in Charlestown.  (*South-Carolina Weekly Gazette*, 29 March 1783)

20.   Maj. Gen. Benjamin Lincoln (1733-1810) was the Continental officer now commanding in the south.  In May 1780 he would be captured with his troops in the capitulation of Charlestown.

21.   A younger son of the Earl of Lauderdale, the Hon John Maitland (?-1781) was Lt. Colonel of the 1st Battalion, 71st (Highland) Regiment.  Having led his battalion in the capture of Savannah, he distinguished himself in the present action at Stono Ferry near Charlestown.  When Prevost withdrew from South Carolina to Savannah, Maitland was left in command of a detachment at Beaufort.  In the defence of Savannah against Franco-revolutionary forces in autumn 1779 he contributed immeasurably to the British success by making a remarkable march from Beaufort to reinforce the garrison.  Ill before he started this movement, he died of malaria a few days after the siege was broken. (Boatner, *Encyclopedia*)

22.   Brig. Gen. Francis McLean (*c.* 1717-1781) was the military commander at Halifax, Nova Scotia.

23.   Commodore Sir George Collier (1738-1795) was one of the most effective naval commanders in North America, as evinced by the Penobscot expedition.  Unable to stand that fool of a naval commander-in-chief, Arbuthnot, who arrived in August 1779, he returned to England.  He died a Vice Admiral of the Blue. (*DNB*)

24.   As a result of his *coup de main* Henry "Light Horse Harry" Lee (1756-1818) gained one of only eight gold medals awarded by Congress during the war.  A decisive and resourceful officer, he would play a consummate, and mostly distinguished, part in the events of 1781 in the Carolinas, commanding, as he did, the American Legion, a corps part infantry, part cavalry.

25.   After an undistinguished naval career Marriot Arbuthnot (1711-1794) had been recently promoted to vice admral of the

blue and was coming out to the North American station as the naval commander-in-chief. A flawed officer past his prime, he was the worst possible choice for the job. There are those in authority — we all have met them — who take pleasure from displaying their power in a negative way by frustrating the will of others. Arbuthnot was just such a man. That there was in his make-up a flaw of this kind is revealed in *The Cornwallis Papers* by the almost grovelling way in which he is addressed by other officers. Negative, inconsistent and unreliable, he would, in short, have tried the patience of a saint — and Clinton was no saint. He relinquished his post in summer 1781.

26.    "81st": perhaps a mistaken reference to the 82nd Regiment.

27.    "Tarleton": for a re-evaluation of this controversial officer, see *The Cornwallis Papers*, i, 154-7.

28.    Anthony Walton White (1750-1803) was Lt. Colonel of the 1st Continental Dragoons. On going to the south he would be worsted by Tarleton in the action at Lenud's Ferry on 6 May 1780.

29.    "Thunder Mountain": more commonly called Dunderberg.

30.    Born in Fifeshire in 1744, James Moncrief, as he signed his surname, had entered the Royal Military College, Woolwich, in 1759, being commissioned an ensign in the Corps of Engineers three years later. Having been severely wounded during the siege of Havana in 1762, he was to serve for many years in the West Indies and North America. On the opening of the Revolutionary War he was present as a captain lieutenant at the capture of Long Island before taking an active part in the Battle of Brandywine and other operations of 1777 and 1778. It was, however, in the south where he gained his fame as an extraordinary military engineer, notably in 1779 in the defence of Savannah, in 1780 in the siege of Charlestown, and subsequently in the formidable fortification of that place. For his services in Georgia he was promoted by brevet to major, and for those at the siege of Charlestown, to lt. colonel. In 1793 he was mortally wounded at the siege of Dunkirk and was buried in Ostend. His name is frequently misspelt by historians. (*DNB*; Boatner, *Encyclopedia*; *Appletons'*)

31.  "11 November": in fact the failed assault took place on 9 October.

32.  A Polish nobleman, Casimir Pulaski (*c.* 1748-1779) was a brigadier general in command of the Continental regiments of dragoons.

33.  The 42nd's embarkation orders were countermanded just before departure.

34.  The transport carrying the Hessian chasseurs was dismasted and carried to England.

35.  Only a reinforcement of 150 men.  The 71st was already serving in the south.

36.  A reference to Althaus's sharpshooters.  When Emmerich's Corps was disbanded at the end of August 1779, the infantry under Captain Althaus was incorporated into the New York Volunteers, which was also serving in the south.

# INDEX

(The letter "n" after a page number indicates the
presence there of biographical or identifying information)